A View from the Wolf's Eye

by Carolyn C. Peterson

with illustrations by Trevor S. Peterson

Isle Royale Natural History Association
Houghton, Michigan

ISBN 978-0-935289-16-9

Library of Congress Catalog Card Number 2008928224

Illustrations by Trevor Peterson

Map by Rolf Peterson

Wolf/Moose graph by Rolf Peterson and John Vucetich

Voices/Choices Diagram by Mike Stockwell, Cranking Graphics

Project Management by Jill Burkland

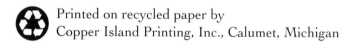

Printed on recycled paper by
Copper Island Printing, Inc., Calumet, Michigan

Contents

*I dedicate this book to my husband, Rolf,
a scientist whose work is an expression
of, not a substitute for, his reverence,
and to Oren Krumm, whose joy continues
to inspire those who knew him.*

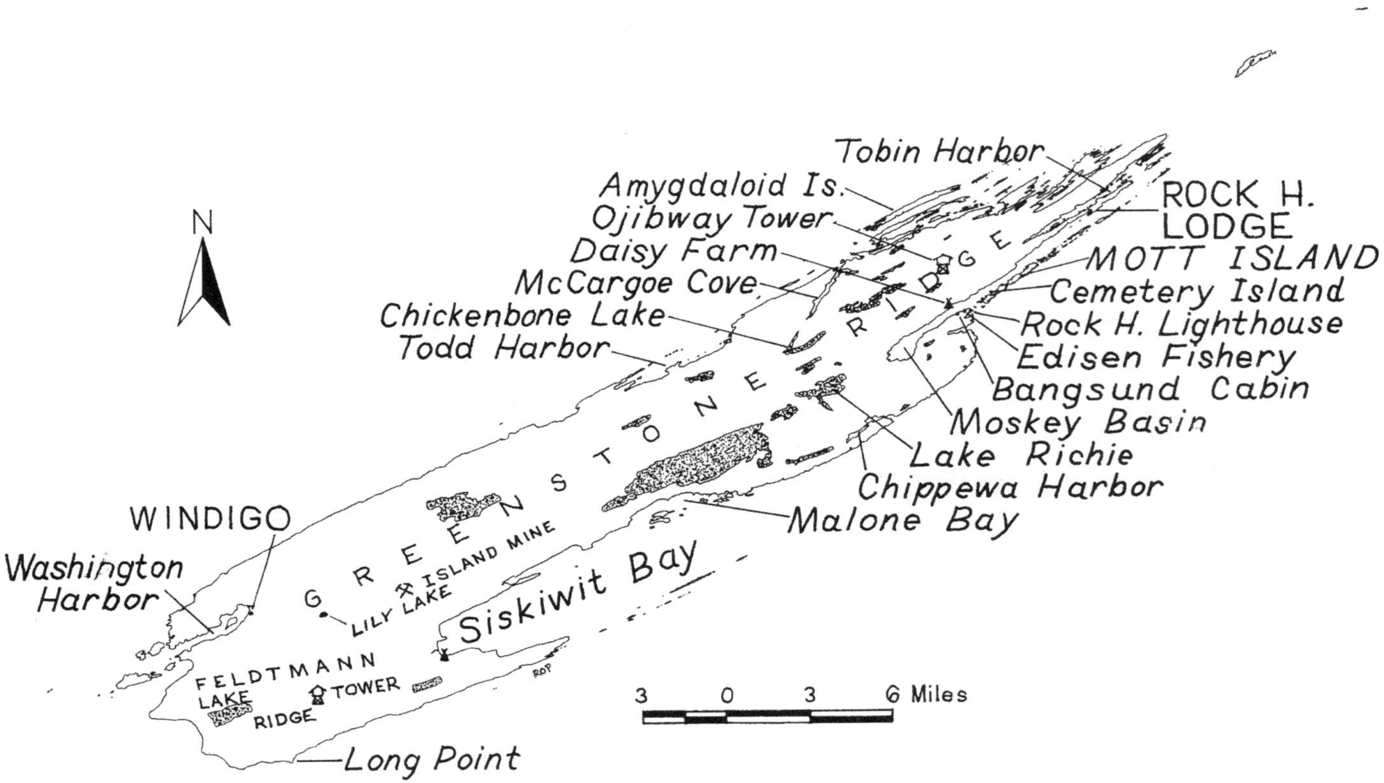

N

Washington
Harbor

WINDIGO

Amygdaloid Is.
Ojibway Tower
Daisy Farm
McCargoe Cove
Chickenbone Lake
Todd Harbor

Tobin Harbor

ROCK H.
LODGE
MOTT ISLAND
Cemetery Island
Rock H. Lighthouse
Edisen Fishery
Bangsund Cabin
Moskey Basin
Lake Richie
Chippewa Harbor
Malone Bay

R   I   D   G   E

G   R   E   E   N   S   T   O   N   E

ISLAND MINE
LILY LAKE
Siskiwit Bay

FELDTMANN
LAKE
RIDGE
TOWER

Long Point

3   0   3   6 Miles

Acknowledgements

Many friends have helped me tell this story. Norma Lee Stuart, Durward L. Allen, Patricia and Peter Van Pelt, Norm Bishop, Thomas A. Waite, Robert and Viola Brown, Robert M. Linn, David Harmon, Paul L. Hayden, Stefan Bechtel, Louise Murie-MacLeod, Tress Lindsay, Dorothy Zeller, Sally Peterson, Susan Burack, Alison Clarke, Debi Davidson, Christine Patten, Debbie Mues, Martha Adkins, Susan Olin, Brian McLaren, William O. Fink, Douglas Barnard, Carl Strang, Bette Mongold, and Ronald Eckoff gave me helpful suggestions and encouragement. David Bezotte helped me track down sources for the quotations I use throughout the book. Marilyn Cooper read and edited the manuscript carefully several times, and I am grateful for all her help. Jill Burkland's faithful shepherding of the whole endeavor was essential. Thank you.

The following young men and women assisted Rolf with the summer fieldwork and shared our table in the past twenty-seven years: John Vanada, Ron Bell, Jim Dietz, Phil Simpson, Tim Lawrence, Mike Wrighthouse, Joseph and Lee Scheidler, Jim Woolington, Phil and Susan Stephens, John Brooks, Mark Cramer, Doug Smith, Mike Phillips, Noel Hanson, Rick Page, Tim Laske, Pat Charmley, Edith Greene, John Boulanger, Jeff Selinger, Ken and Lynn Risenhoover, Peter Zavell, Tim Ackerman, Joanne Thurber, Dan Fehringer, Drew Metzger, Brian McLaren, Mary Hindelang, Tony Schwaller, Chris Fink, John and Leah Vucetich, Marco Heurich, Joe Zanon, Willow Foster, Jenny Mahan, Cindy Carter, Menna Jones, Jeff Plakke, Seth Maefsky, Boerge Wahl, Marcel Potvin, Justin Gude, Anne Chouinard, Ellen Jedrey, Philip DeWitt, Greg Burkhart, Ken Mills, Nathan Hambel, Jason Deutsch, Elizabeth Clement, Emily Grosvenor, Sam Gardner, and Matt Abbotts.

Sources for (almost) all quotations can be found in the list of sources at the end of the book.

The most important characters in my story are Rolf, who keeps trying to teach me to be attentive to detail, and our sons Jeremy and Trevor, who continue to renew my faith in the big picture.

Introduction

I have a friend who prefaces all stories of her life by saying, "Do you want to know the truth, or the truth as I remember it?" Mindful of the fact that all my memories are subjective (I have kept a daily journal since 1972, however), I offer this memoir, my story of more than thirty-five summers on Isle Royale. Assisting my husband in wolf-moose research, I fell in love with his study area, which has since served as a summer nursery, home base, and launching pad for our sons and a listening point for my spirit. Grateful for the blessings of nature, family, and Isle Royale visitors, I hope that my experiences will inspire others to seek, enjoy, and preserve the remaining wild places on this planet, including the unlimited reservoir that is the human heart.

Part One: 1970s
Research Assistant — Learning

The most beautiful and most profound emotion we can experience is the sensation of the mystical. It is the sower of all true science. He to whom this emotion is a stranger, who can no longer stand rapt in awe, is as good as dead. To know that what is impenetrable to us really exists, manifesting itself as the highest wisdom and the most radiant beauty which our dull faculties can comprehend only in their most primitive forms—this knowledge, this feeling is at the center of true religiousness.
— Albert Einstein (qtd. in Barnett, p. 117)

If you can see the profile of a wolf's head in the outline of Lake Superior, Isle Royale is the lean and hungry eye of that wolf, and when you stand on the island's basalt backbone, you are connected to some of Earth's oldest rock. Oblivious to human measures of success and failure and to colonization by various flora and fauna, the island remains steady and strong, an effective antidote for modern malaise and a testament to nature's healing processes.

Twenty miles from the nearest shore, Isle Royale is a remarkable wildlife study area, for the number of mammalian species is limited to those that can fly, swim in very cold water, or cross on the ice. The fifteen mammals that currently occupy the island, including moose, wolf, beaver, red fox, otter, snowshoe hare, pine marten, and red squirrel, are essentially captive. Isle Royale provides a small and protected cast of characters whose interactions are relatively simple to monitor and understand.

Moose arrived on Isle Royale early in the twentieth century, probably swimming from Canada, but there is a story, not yet authenticated, that they were brought to Isle Royale by a group of hunting enthusiasts from Minnesota. Without predators, moose

1

thrived in a heavenly garden of favorite foods, but by the 1930s they had overpopulated the island and were starving. An attempt to move moose from Isle Royale to the Upper Peninsula of Michigan was unsuccessful, though it produced some entertaining movie footage. Similarly, imported captive wolves, instead of limiting moose numbers as intended, became pests around human establishments on Isle Royale and had to be removed. In the late 1940s, wild wolves appeared on Isle Royale, presumably having crossed on the ice from Canada during a particularly cold winter. That wolves would kill all the moose and then start eating park visitors seemed a real possibility at the time, when wolves were still feared and hated in our country. Durward L. Allen of Purdue University, fascinated by this natural predator-prey experiment on Isle Royale, procured the funds to begin a long-term study. Since 1958 the ups and downs of the moose and wolf populations have been carefully recorded, and the findings have fascinated people all over the world.

The particular magic of Isle Royale captivated me in 1969, on my first visit, for it was here that I fell in love. As a member of a spur-of-the-moment, end-of-the-summer backpacking adventure with seven other counselors from St. Paul YMCA Camp Widjiwagan near Ely, Minnesota, I met Rolf Peterson. My first impression of him was indelible—always at the rear of our procession, often on his knees, photographing a caterpillar or spider web unnoticed by the rest of us. A broad-vista, whizz-bang type myself, I was fascinated by Rolf's quiet respect for all nature, especially the bit players.

Love was not on my agenda at that point in my life. A product of both the idealistic 1960s and the Protestant work ethic, I was searching for a meaningful way to give something back to a world that had invested so much in me. As a tot I had accompanied Mom, a "red feather lady," when she solicited donations for the Community Chest in Duluth, and my hardworking and meticulously honest father had taught me to admire his heroes, Meriwether Lewis, Albert Schweitzer, and Abraham Lincoln, men of vision, courage, and action. At home, in school, church, and Girl Scouts, I learned that work, whether paid or voluntary, is satisfying, even enjoyable. At Wellesley College the motto *Non Ministrari, Sed Ministrare* (not to be ministered unto, but to minister) reinforced the practical lessons I had learned as a child, and I was eager for a mission.

In the spring of 1969, as a junior in college, I had been asked to help lead the graduating seniors to their commencement exercises. It was a memorable day. The guest speaker, Edward Brooke, a liberal senator from Massachusetts, used many statistics to admonish the new graduates to be patient, to proceed slowly in attempting to change the world, to right the seemingly intractable wrongs. He received polite, unenthusiastic applause. The next speaker, graduating senior Hillary Rodham, challenged Senator Brooke point by point and called for more humane, more progressive political action. "For too long," she said, "those who lead us have viewed politics as the art of the possible. The challenge that faces us now is to practice politics as the art of making possible what appears to be impossible." She spoke extemporaneously; I have always wondered what she had planned to say that day. It was 1969, and students were fired up to bring peace and justice to this world in one generation. Hillary received a seven-minute standing ovation, and it was exciting and a little frightening to be part of the crowd. My shift from Goldwater Republican to anti-war Democrat came a year later, when the United States bombed Cambodia.

My frustration as a college student was that I didn't know where to dig in, how to be part of the solution. I was idealistic and young; I wanted a big project, to be the fisherman instead of a knot in the net. My friends all seemed to have been called to various careers, but I had changed majors three times and was floundering. Having grown up with my parents' accounts of the Great Depression and its constraints, I couldn't complain about the overabundance of choices available to me. Instead of focusing my interests, college had expanded my horizons, a gift which, at that stage of my life, I would have gladly exchanged for a marketable skill and a job offer.

I found a temporary solution to my unjelled plans—the Peace Corps. My older brother had served in this program on the north coast of Borneo, where he and his wife taught language, art, history, math, and science to Malay and Chinese children. Inspired by his enthusiastic reports, I enrolled in several anthropology, political science, and international economics courses, and I resolved not to let anything interfere with my plan; my brother had warned me that if I had strong ties to home I would not survive the first few mosquito bites.

But now Rolf Peterson filled my mind—blond, blue-eyed, quietly strong, humble, self-assured, and competent and comfortable in the woods. I clearly saw his beautiful soul. As I flew back to Boston for my senior year, I decided to write Rolf a letter at the University of

Minnesota, Duluth (UMD), simply telling him he was a credit to the human race. My letter crossed a similar one from him, a coincidence that should have given me pause, but it would take me another thirty years to become open to the possibility of miracles. We continued to write, sharing our opinions about families, politics, religion, our deepest hopes and dreams. My mother had given me my best writing lesson years before, while I composed a sympathy note: write from the heart. By Christmas, my center of gravity had shifted; I was somewhat peeved that my Peace Corps dream would not come true, yet I was certain that I would follow this Scandinavian nature-lover anywhere. It was satisfying for me, an unfocused generalist, to support Rolf, so well-suited to his chosen field of wildlife research. Rolf's dream was noble and large enough for two people; I happily exchanged my amorphous goal for a concrete project, and some of my freedom for the love and support of a life companion.

Through canoe trips in the Boundary Waters Canoe Area in northern Minnesota, Ontario's Quetico Provincial Park, and Canada's barren lands, Rolf had grown to love northern wilderness. Born and raised in Minneapolis, he had always dreamed of living closer to the woods. As a child he had clipped an article with wildlife photos by Dave Mech, who was studying wolves and moose on Isle Royale. In November 1969, while a senior at UMD, Rolf saw a television documentary that included a segment on the Isle Royale wolf-moose research directed by Durward L. Allen. Rolf watched the credits, found Dr. Allen's address at Purdue University, and wrote a letter of inquiry. Rolf lives in faith that things generally work out for the best, an attitude richly rewarded when Dr. Allen offered to direct him in a PhD project on the Isle Royale wolves.

The island would be the focus of Rolf's life for several years, and he seemed to think I would make a good helpmate. During spring vacation, Rolf asked my parents for my hand and, upon giving an acceptable answer to Daddy's question, "Do you love her?" was welcomed into the family. I have always felt Mom and Dad loved Rolf, a good feeling to have during the inevitable doldrums of a marriage: were I to leave Rolf, I would find little sympathy at home. We set a wedding date for September, exactly one year from the day we had met.

Rolf spent the summer before we were married on Isle Royale, getting the feel of the place and searching for remains of moose killed by wolves during the previous winter. Long streamers of flagging had been dropped from the research plane to help the ground crew locate carcasses spotted from the air. That summer, and in the next several summers, a lot of flagging was found—one of Rolf's first conclusions was that the person who plots the "kills" on the map in winter from the airplane ought to collect the bones in summer. Kill sites are as difficult to map accurately from a circling airplane in winter as they are to find on the ground in summer; Rolf was eager to do both.

We were married in Duluth and had a brief honeymoon up the Gunflint Trail in northeastern Minnesota. In some ways we barely knew each other. Courtship by correspondence had enabled us to share our philosophical concerns; our compatibility in other respects would have to be worked out. With a lifetime ahead, we resolved to make our marriage thrive; our parents provided ample proof that long-term commitments are possible, even joyful. Several coincidences made our adjustment to marriage easy. We were both the youngest of three children, showered with attention and accustomed to receiving. Raised by confident, happy parents and older siblings, we took love for granted. Our parents were identical in age, with our fathers seven years older than our mothers and, being survivors of the Great Depression, grateful for material security. Our families had taken us to church (Rolf was Lutheran, I Congregationalist/Episcopalian), where we learned the vocabulary of praise, compassion, and forgiveness. Finally, we had both spent the first twenty-one years of our lives under the same house number: 3512. Whether "fate" had a hand in our introduction was something I would ponder for years.

We drove a rented van containing a few possessions to West Lafayette, Indiana. Neither of us wanted to own a car—at the age of twenty-one, Rolf had paddled more miles than he had driven, and we both have always had ethical problems with the automobile. We had no savings, and bicycles provided sufficient transportation, for there aren't many places flatter than the Purdue campus. We lived in married student housing, about as unadorned as such places can be, built after World War II with streets named for war heroes like Nimitz, Marshall, and Halsey. No car, no TV, no phone—we were unencumbered and happy.

My first real job, after seventeen years of formal education, was to shepherd the corporate records collection of the Krannert Business School Library. Try as I might, I simply could not get excited about that locked roomful of glossy annual reports. It was a long way from the Peace Corps, and I spent many hours walking around Purdue's experimental cornfields, wrestling with that familiar question, "What should I do with my life?" As an employee, I was able to take university courses without charge, and I enrolled in two education classes. Just to be looking forward again was a relief; with my dreams unleashed, reality was bearable. Instead of exploring my box, I plotted an escape from it.

In January 1971, Rolf drove north with Dr. Allen to Minnesota, and from Eveleth they flew in a small plane to Isle Royale for the seven-week winter study. Their landing field was the ice of Washington Harbor, their base of operations the ranger bunkhouse at Windigo. The Isle Royale wolves had never been handled by researchers and were spared the hazards proximity to "civilization" brings: bullets, poison, untended traps, motor vehicles, and competition with people for prey and territory. The low point for wolves in the United States occurred just after World War II, when people added to their arsenal of anti-wolf weaponry the small light aircraft that had proliferated during the war.

Pilot Don Murray was a pivotal character in the winter studies for eighteen years. A truck driver from Mt. Iron, Minnesota, his flying experience came as a crop duster. It was a tremendous privilege to be the observer in Don Murray's small Aeronca Champ airplane; it was also a terrific responsibility. Rolf's first challenge would be to control his stomach during tight circles, the pilot's specialty. Some of Rolf's predecessors had vomited at the sight of the plane each morning!

Don Murray was a superb pilot, and Rolf trusted him completely, which helped in the matter of stomach-control. But more than this, Don taught Rolf to glean information from tracks seen from the air, to distinguish moose, fox, and wolf tracks and to reconstruct the action of a hunt that had occurred during the night. The wolves were accustomed to Don's flying technique (he was careful not to surprise or crowd them), so Rolf was certain the behavior he observed was natural.

In spite of Rolf's faith in Don Murray, I was a basket-case of worry and loneliness in our quiet apartment at Purdue. I was

6

surprised and disgusted by my dependence on Rolf; is this what love does to a person? In four short months, I had become a wet rag! It helped to believe that Rolf's work was important, that many people were genuinely interested in wolves, and that the wolves were worthy of this notice. The Isle Royale study was teaching people all over the world that wolves are selective predators who cull the old, young, and sick moose, leaving the mature and healthy ones to reproduce. By keeping the moose numbers down, wolves unwittingly protect the forest by preventing moose from devastating their own food supply. Nature's ways are complex and awe-inspiring, and Rolf, with his careful, thorough habits, was a terrific scientist. Focusing on the island and its lessons helped calm my fears about Rolf's safety. It was then that I came upon an adage by Antoine de Saint Exupéry that has resonated throughout my life: "Love does not consist in gazing at one another but in looking outward together in the same direction" (p. 229).

The best way for me to help Rolf was to be happy myself. As newlyweds, we needed money, and my best service was to tend those corporate records. But in the winters of 1973 and 1974, I went home to Duluth and enrolled at UMD to obtain certification to teach high school history and economics. Mom and Dad indulged me with the same top-notch room, board, and laundry service they had provided for the first eighteen years of my life, and I put all my energy into student teaching, loving every minute of it.

Had I been invited to participate in Rolf's first winter studies, I would certainly have jumped at the chance. But Dr. Allen and Don Murray were adamant, back in the days when men could be adamant about such things: *no women!* Men are different when they are on their own; at winter study Dr. Allen, Don Murray, and Rolf were finding freedom and camaraderie somewhat similar to what I had experienced at a women's college. With Rolf's life dependent on the pilot and his career dependent on Dr. Allen, I decided to lie low. At the time, I resented the exclusion, but in retrospect I am glad my wings were clipped; I was learning to put silver linings in my clouds, arguably life's most important skill.

Dorothy Allen had been putting up with these winter separations for fourteen years and assured me that I would, some day, see advantages in the time alone. I was skeptical and wondered about the strength of their marriage. I wallowed in pain and self-pity: how unfair that the best seven weeks of Rolf's annual calendar were the most difficult for me! But Dorothy Allen was right, and each winter I learned to stand on my own feet. My loneliness nudged me out of our little apartment, and the new people I met expanded my horizons and stretched my heart. In March, Rolf and I came together in strength.

Rolf sent word from the island by letter, our familiar mode of communication, and I was fascinated to learn each January how the wolves were organized, how many pups had survived, and what shape the moose population was in. During the early 1970s, a series of severe winters caused the moose numbers to plummet. For moose, deep snow that confines them and covers their food is more troublesome than cold temperatures, and wolves, aided by crusts on the snow, take advantage of their weakened condition. Rolf began measuring snow and searching weather records to relate moose welfare to snow characteristics.

Apparently because of the bountiful supply of weak, starved moose, the wolf population increased dramatically in the first years of Rolf's vigil. When wolves feed on animals as large as moose, fifteen or twenty individuals can crowd around the dinner table, so packs can be large. For several years in a row in the 1970s, the East Pack produced litters of as many as seven pups. Also, with moose so easy to kill, wolf packs did not need to maintain large territories—why bother to run to the other end of the island when dinner can be had at the next drainage? Rich wolves hang out with each other and chew the fat, unlike their human counterparts, who enlarge their ecological footprint. When a pack's territory shrinks, vacant space is available to colonists. Although most wolves live in packs, there is generally a disgruntled wolf that would rather leave its family than put up with the pecking order in a pack. (Wolf packs are dominated by a pair of autocrats, an alpha male and female, who usually do all the breeding.) When there are vacant areas in a range, a lone female can team up with a male to begin a new pack and, with enough to eat, keep a litter of pups alive. In 1970 there were two packs on the island; ten years later there were five.

Winter fieldwork was centered on the wolves and was mostly done from the air, with few people participating, but the summer project was much different, involving a larger crew and based at the east end of the island. Typically, Dr. Allen's graduate student directed the summer operation, and most of Rolf's predecessors had brought their wives. My first summer on the island was 1971. It didn't start out well. Rolf and a field assistant, Jim Dietz, now head of a conservation biology program at the University of Maryland, hiked as a team, and I stayed behind at Bangsund Cabin. The Bangsund family had based their fishery at the cabin on Rock Harbor across from Daisy Farm Campground in the 1940s and 1950s before lampreys decimated the heavily harvested lake trout population. Jack Bangsund had died in this cabin in 1959, and Dave Mech, Dr. Allen's first Isle Royale student, received National Park Service (NPS) permission to house his summer field operation here. Wolf-moose researchers have lived at Bangsund Cabin ever since.

I was an experienced camper (my parents had taken me on canoe trips in Minnesota's Boundary Waters Canoe Area since I was four, and long canoe trips at camp had sharpened my skills), yet I found life in an old fisherman's cabin to be difficult. This was not the log cabin on the cover of an L.L. Bean catalog, with varnished pine logs and a stone hearth. The ambience of Bangsund Cabin in 1971 was (and is!) "dated utilitarian." The logs had long since been painted light green on the inside, and to keep out the wind, tarpaper had been nailed to the outside. The rocking chair "upholstery" was oily and dingy, the curtains faded and dusty, and the floor badly atilt. The roof leaked, and spiders, deer mice, bats, and garter snakes passed at will through the gaps between the log walls and the warped floor. Imagined horrors lurked behind cabinets, and it took years for me to muster courage to probe the darkest corners. To make matters worse, I was often alone. While Rolf and Jim were out on adventures, I was lonesome and bored, even frightened, at the cabin. Once again, that Peace Corps alternative tempted me.

I told my parents about some of the cabin's deficiencies, and my mother, delighted to frequent junk shops in Duluth, over the coming years provided many pots and pans and nearly all of our kitchen gadgets. Mom had always been a masterful packer, and her talents reached their peak as she squeezed binoculars, pecans, bug hats, potholders, a stove-top waffle iron, and canning supplies into a small box. One memorable item she sent was a garden trowel of unusual design. I had used it several times when I received a letter from home asking about the potato masher she had tucked into a recent care package.

Joe Scheidler and Jim Woolington, summer assistants in 1974 and 1975, wrote this poem about Bangsund Cabin:

A home that's built from pulp sticks
Which were washed up on the shore,
Snuggled in the northern woods,
Who could ask for more?
Now it may not look too fancy,
'Least when compared to the homes we know today,
But if it were mine to change it,
I'd leave it just this way.
Now it ain't got no electricity or plumbin',
None of that stuff,
But it's got a roof that sheds the rain,
And I reckon that's enough.
A moose might peek in its window,
And the fox and snowshoe hare
Might romp around right close to it
As if it wasn't there.
There's a brood of black ducks just outside,
A deer mouse on the floor,
Garter snake behind the stove . . .
Hard tellin' what all more.
I guess it was originally built here
To fulfill some fisherman's need.
But I like to think that nature planned it
. . . and growed it from a seed!

It took some effort for me to love all nature's parts as thoroughly and effortlessly as Rolf did. I accepted critters outside where they belonged but was frustrated not to be able to pick my cabin mates. The pitter-patter/thump of mice in the ceiling above our bed kept me awake at night, and in early morning light I couldn't take my eyes off spiders, some real, some imagined, on our chipboard ceiling. One bad day, as I walked out the front door, something fell on my head and encircled my neck. Instinctively, I grabbed the thing and flung it out into the lake with all the strength of my adrenaline-pumped body, and then learned that garter snakes are accomplished swimmers. I knew the snake was harmless and was merely enjoying the warm sun on the doorjamb, but fear is often irrational, and it took some time for my jitters to subside.

Another new experience was operating powerboats. My first solo adventure in the old wooden "Wolf" with twin 20-hp motors nearly ended in disaster when I forgot which motor was permanently stuck in forward gear. Having turned off the wrong one and heading straight for shore at a fast clip, I had to hop over the windshield and jump into the shallow water to keep the hull from crunching on our rocky beach.

Neighbors were a Godsend. Pete and Laura Edisen operated a fishery a quarter-mile away, and I used the trail Pete had made years before, when he and his brother shared a shack near the Bangsund Cabin and courted Laura, who lived with her parents, also fishermen, near the Rock Harbor Lighthouse. Pete and Laura were the most generous, hospitable, friendly folks I had ever known, and how I needed those cups of coffee in their cozy kitchen! Pete had been born in Norway and recalled "the old country" fondly, yet he spoke with equal reverence about Isle Royale. He showed no favoritism with respect to humans and other animals; in fact, he had a wonderfully positive attitude toward just about everything. It felt good to be near Pete.

The Edisens had no children. Pete told me that as a small child, Laura had been present at the birth of her half-brother and had been so terrified that she resolved never to have a child. Love will have its outlet, however, and Pete and Laura bestowed their affection on those around them—relatives, friends, and neighbors. During one of my visits, Laura taught me how to bake bread, and to this day I follow her recipes. Kneading "Laura's bread" still brings warmth to my heart; her spirit is alive and well.

11

Laura Edisen's Dark Bread

1 T dry yeast (1 pkg) dissolved in 1/2 C warm water
2 C warm water
1/4 C butter, margarine, or oil
1/3 C sugar
1/2 T salt
1/4 C molasses
2 C whole wheat or rye flour
about 5 C white flour

Dissolve yeast in 1/2 cup warm water. Heat 2 cups water, shortening, sugar, salt, and molasses. Add the dark flour and stir well. Add yeast/water mix, making sure you don't kill the yeast with too much heat. Gradually stir in as much white flour as possible, then turn out onto a board and knead for 10 minutes until the dough is no longer sticky. Hopefully, it is still nice and warm. Place in a greased bowl and let rise in a warm place until double, about 1 1/4 hours (the pilot light in the propane stove at Bangsund Cabin creates a perfect environment). Punch down dough, form into two balls, and let them rest for 10 minutes. Grease two bread pans, form each ball of dough into a loaf (find a picture in any cookbook). Let rise in pans for an hour or so, until double.

Bake at 350 degrees for 30 to 35 minutes. Brush with butter when fresh out of the oven.

Laura Edisen's Cinnamon Bread

1 T dry yeast dissolved in 1/4 C warm water
2 1/8 C warm water
1/3 C sugar
1/4 C butter
1/2 T salt
6 C flour, approximately

Mix ingredients as described in the previous recipe. After the first rising, roll each half of dough into a rectangle and brush with melted butter. Sprinkle a mixture of 2 teaspoons cinnamon and 3/4 cup sugar over the dough, then roll into loaves. Bake at 350 degrees for 30 to 35 minutes.

Pete and Laura had not received much formal education, but they had learned something far more important: happiness comes not from pursuit. Instead of wanting to change the world, they were grateful for what's already here. Rather than grouse about bad luck, they used their good minds to see the beauty in all situations and their hearts to serve other people. Pete's positive spin on stories and Laura's generous hospitality meant more than all the education I had come to worship in college. I had thought of the cracks in the cabin walls as a problem to be solved; Pete and Laura taught me to see the light that comes through the cracks.

Despite the best neighbors imaginable, by July of that first summer my impatience with idleness was greater than my apprehension about Rolf and Jim's pace, and I asked to go along. Rolf had purchased lightweight camping equipment, and with reasonable loads we left the trails and used a topographical map, aerial photos, and compasses to explore areas of interest. The work was manageable because the guys carried more than their fair share, and since we stopped whenever a bone was spotted, I kept my eyes peeled for any and all excuses to stop. The good times had begun! As I followed the man I loved over ridges and through swamps, I fell under Isle Royale's spell.

One of my best memories of 1971 was learning to recognize some bird songs. Bird identification by sight alone is a challenge after the trees leaf out in June, and even in May I had trouble looking up with binoculars while carrying a heavy backpack. Rolf had learned many calls from Jack Hofslund, his ornithology professor at UMD, and he suggested I master a few songs at

OVENBIRD

a time. We found Roger Tory Peterson's renditions to be most helpful, and soon I was able to make sense of the morning chorus in early summer. Winter wrens (the long-winded, ebullient singers of the boreal forest), ovenbirds ("teacher teacher teacher teacher"), black-throated green warblers ("zzeee zzeee zzeee zo zzeee"), red-eyed vireos ("see me? here I am, over here," or, as a preacher: "do you hear me? are you listening? do you get it? can you do it?"), and white-throated sparrows ("oh poor Sam Peabody Peabody Peabody") were the first to become familiar. Those species that took the longest time to identify have become indelible in my mind. I remember hearing a "robin with a scratchy throat" on the Island Mine Trail, and when we took a break and scanned the trees overhead with binoculars I was delighted to see a scarlet tanager! Each spring I expect a redstart behind Daisy Farm Campground, a hermit thrush on the Greenstone Ridge near Ojibway Tower, and a blackburnian warbler, winter wren, and swainson's thrush behind the cabin. I look forward to annual reunions with these old friends, and a few unrecognizable songs add excitement and keep me humble.

Learning to recognize birds by their songs was my first step from tourist to native. An aspiring world traveler, I was surprised to discover the pleasures of getting to know one place really well. Familiarity casts out fear and fosters connection, and natural areas bring me humble joy because I take no credit for what I see, nor do I think of ways to "improve" things. Public spaces put me in the audience, along with other people. A landscape need not be dramatic to touch the spirit. The Grand Canyon, even Denali's vast expanse, has not made my heart throb as does a muddy beaver pond on Isle Royale, where I know some of the creatures and remember that several years ago the pond was dry. Sitting by that pond, amid kingbirds and warblers, aware that evolution has worked for millions of years to produce what I see today, I am in love with life, excited and genuinely happy to be part of the whole system. My role, a witness, feels significant. "Stand still and look until you really see," says an old poster on our cabin wall.

Another advantage to getting to know the close-to-home landscapes is that the experiences are affordable and repeatable. When I have not invested a lot of time and energy to reach my destination and the planet has not been harmed by my activity, I can begin to reap the profits immediately. Even more important, as soon as I realize that the joy I feel on Isle Royale is what Thoreau found at Walden Pond and John Muir among California's coastal redwood forests, I no longer need to visit other people's beautiful places. While Isle Royale may seem a country church next to Yosemite's mother cathedral, spirit is alive in both places, and frequent attendance pays off.

A Norwegian reminded me that we find beauty wherever we choose to see it. He seemed surprised that I found the mountains and fjords of his country breathtakingly beautiful. "Beautiful?" he exclaimed, "You think these mountains are beautiful? My ancestors nearly starved trying to farm this place!" When I asked him what sort of landscape he considered beautiful, his eyes lit up as he replied, "The prairies of Nebraska." To appreciate beauty, one's stomach must be full.

Isle Royale's charm is subtle and undramatic, but I find its humility appealing. When I approach Isle Royale with time and curiosity, opening my heart and senses, the place speaks to me in a clear voice. The island is, in some ways, a wounded landscape; it has been mined, logged, and burned, yet it is a testament to nature's power to heal itself. I feel blessed to be alive in such a place, a part of nature, as good as all the other players. Isle Royale's wholeness is a balm, a reminder that we are forgiven for our mistakes, and a challenge to "go, and sin no more."

Isle Royale has taught me not to make comparisons between natural areas. The island, like every other spot on this planet, is doing the best it can. Comparing Isle Royale to places with higher mountains and taller trees simply makes me unhappy. Like the Edisens, I'm rewarded when I make the effort to see the good in all things.

While I enjoyed getting to know Isle Royale, Rolf was a bit uneasy about his project. He was the most recent in a fairly long line of Isle Royale wolf-moose researchers, and he was afraid that the big questions had already been answered. It seemed that some sort of balance had been established, with the wolves keeping the moose population under control. Dr. Allen's faith was helpful—he convinced Rolf to wait and watch.

And Rolf did not have to wait long, for the winters of 1969, 1971, and 1972 were very difficult for moose. Because of their high numbers and the exceptionally deep snow, moose died faster than wolves could kill them. Winter browse, especially balsam fir, was chewed to a frazzle, and desperate moose broke off tops of young trees to feed themselves. (Bulls are especially susceptible to long, hard winters, having spent much of the autumn preoccupied with the rut, competing with other bulls and tending the cows.) Thus the first new idea to surface during Rolf's tour of duty on Isle Royale was that to accurately describe predator-prey relationships on Isle Royale, one must monitor the weather. Exceptional weather jolts the whole system.

To uncover more of the mystery of Isle Royale, we had to do a better job of finding dead moose. In 1972, Rolf hired two field assistants to work as a second team, scouring the island for bones. On one of our trips, an overnight to Chippewa Harbor, we found a dozen carcasses. All too often, wolves had not yet discovered the dead moose or had eaten only the "soft parts." With prey so vulnerable, sometimes it was easier to kill another moose than to chew on a frozen carcass. At one site we found five legs. Finding carcasses was much more exciting than "processing" them when wolves were not cleaning them up. Skinning leg bones and looking for arthritis in the pelvis or necrosis in the jaws is messy and smelly work, especially when the knife edge and saw blade are worn. In those years, I was paid as a half-time assistant, and that had a real advantage—I could always manage to be the recording secretary and sit upwind when a horrid-smelling, maggot-infested dead moose needed to be processed.

Another way to locate more moose carcasses was to come earlier in spring. I took temporary jobs at Purdue so I could accompany Rolf as soon as ice was out of harbors and NPS boats were operating. In early May, there was no underbrush hiding moose bones, and wolves were still using park trails. At the same time, bushwhacking was as easy as it ever gets on the island. It was frustrating not to have more hours in a day; we felt we were racing against the new vegetation poking its way up through last year's brittle, brown leaves.

Spring is the season of the young and hardy, the newborns and the veterans of the harsh northern winter. Like cocky youngsters, Rolf and I were sometimes foolish. One 80-degree day in early May, we pushed ourselves to reach the shady relief of the sugar maple forest at the west end of the island, completely forgetting that leafless trees provide no shade. Another morning we awoke in a collapsed tent and laughed in surprise when we poked our heads out the door to find that three inches of heavy, wet snow had fallen during the night.

As if our packs were not heavy enough, Rolf kept thinking up reasons to collect additional bones. In 1970, a jaw would suffice. By 1972, we were collecting both jaws and a metatarsus bone (the lower rear leg bone in a moose, the long bone in your foot) and all arthritic joints. By 1979, we were bringing home the skulls, too, and if antlers were attached, this could be a fifty-pound load. Our packs usually weighed more at the end of a trip than at the start.

Dead moose turned up in odd places. One stumbled into an old water-filled mine pit behind Daisy Farm Campground. Rolf, leaning over a log he had placed across the opening of the pit, worked on this carcass with an audience of interested campers. Another unlucky moose was electrocuted by a dangling power line that ran, at that time, from Mott Island to Ojibway Tower. We camped near the carcass for several days, expecting the wolves to appear, and we ended our vigil when we thought the carcass was too decomposed to be of any use to the wolves. We checked the site periodically and, weeks later, were astonished to learn that hungry wolves have no problem eating rotten meat. Occasionally a moose died from exhaustion and trauma with a front leg caught in the crotch of a tree. Prodded by hunger, these moose paid dearly for their overreaching. The most colorful carcass I remember made its surprise appearance twenty feet off the end of our dock one July. When a moose breaks through the ice in early spring or late fall, it sinks and remains on the bottom until it reaches a particular stage of decomposition, at which point it resurfaces. We towed the orange, purple, and green mass to a beach a few hundred yards away where the gulls and foxes made quick work of the remains. Soon thereafter we began to filter our drinking water.

Although Rolf's research was supposedly focused on wolves, we seemed to spend most of our time with dead moose. After seeing repeatedly what wolves could do to a thousand-pound moose, I developed a great respect for the elusive predators. I also understood wolves' need to be left alone. We did not want to intrude on a den or summer home, called a rendezvous site, lest the wolves move, perhaps losing a pup or two because of the disruption. Feeding a litter of pups during the summer is difficult because moose are strong and can escape into open water. Our business was to study the dynamics of undisturbed populations, not to see how closely wolves tolerate humans. Our rare sightings of wolves were thrilling but usually unsatisfying: we see wolf, wolf runs.

I had my first good look at Isle Royale wolves at Lily Lake in 1972. We had just finished breakfast and stood in the trees, looking over the lake, when we heard howling. Within seconds, two wolves appeared, the only two recognizable wolves on the island at that time, the big black alpha male of the West Pack and the small gray alpha female. They didn't see us and walked along the bog mat, appearing to enjoy a little time to themselves. My heart pounded with excitement; I felt no fear, just exhilaration to be privy to their morning outing. The sight was a gift, especially valuable because we had waited so long for it.

Only once in the 1970s were we able to watch wolves for an extended period. Seated on a ridge high above the drained beaver pond where the East Pack had a rendezvous site, we imagined they were unaware of our presence; we certainly did all we could to prevent detection. Rolf did not use his camera because of its noisy shutter; instead, we recorded their howling. Seven pups were born in that pack in 1973, and we watched them at play, attacking a birch log and wrestling with one another. Wolves leave their den after several weeks, but the pups do not travel with the pack for the first few months. When an adult came home with food in its stomach, it was greeted with wild exuberance. Pups nipped at the corners of the adult's mouth, causing the adult to regurgitate, and the chunks of meat were gobbled up by the hungry youngsters. Seven pups is a large number to feed, and we noticed that one of the pups was not given a fair share. This small pup, which won our sympathy and the nickname "7-up," was also the underdog in every wrestling match. The pack moved after just a week to another, less exposed site, and we were never again able to watch them at a den or rendezvous site.

Although we seldom saw wolves, we learned a great deal from their howling, and in the 1970s, when the packs were well-fed and growing, we heard group howls frequently. By 1975, I actually became irritated with the howling that played havoc with our sleep. Rolf had borrowed a super-sensitive microphone from Purdue, and he mounted it on a tripod and covered it with a plastic bag to protect it from heavy dew at night. Whenever wolves howled, Rolf hopped out of the tent, removed the bag, and stood still, swarmed by mid-summer hordes of mosquitoes or chilled by autumn air, keeping the bag quiet while I pushed the tape recorder buttons inside the tent. After repeating this sequence half a dozen times in a night, we groaned when the wolves howled. Little did we know that we wouldn't have this opportunity again for twenty-five years!

Another aspect of summer fieldwork involved keeping records on all live moose we saw. Behavior wasn't our major focus, but moose are fascinating creatures, quite tolerant of curious humans. When they choose, they can silently disappear, lifting their long legs to clear windfalls and underbrush. Humans are clumsy and noisy by comparison. If startled, however, a moose can crash through the woods, which usually sends people bolting in the opposite direction.

Often, the best way for a moose to avoid detection is to keep still, letting us plod past with our eyes on the ground, packs creaking, and minds preoccupied.

Many people have made fun of the appearance of a moose. The "committee" that designed this creature was not headed by an artist, perhaps, but there are reasons for all of its parts. Its eyes have horizontal pupils, helpful in nearly 300-degree vigilance, and are protected by eyelashes "that Hollywood would die for," says Rolf. Valves in the soft, bulbous nose can close off the air passage when a moose feeds underwater, and the convoluted air passages inside that big nose help the animal keep cool in summer and warm in winter. The large ears can be rotated 180 degrees, antlers are hugely attractive to cows, and the legs and feet are formidable weapons. The bell, or dewlap, enlarges a bull's silhouette in the fall and is also of olfactory significance during the rut when bulls dig shallow pits, mark them with urine, and rub their bells therein. Even the slow pace that is the norm for moose has a purpose: keeping cool in summer and conserving energy in winter. The large size of the animal also helps it stay warm during a wet, cold spring when it is often plagued by hair loss due to winter ticks. In one respect, however, I think evolution has shortchanged the moose. The animal could really use a tail to whisk away pesky flies. Rolf says the moose is a relative newcomer to the Western Hemisphere, having migrated across the land bridge from Siberia to Alaska; perhaps its tail froze off en route. Certainly, a tail would be a difficult appendage to keep warm in winter.

Each summer, we were particularly interested in the proportion of calves in our moose sightings. After the deep-snow winters of the early 1970s, calves were small in both number and size. Yearlings were so small that we sometimes mistook them for calves. Those young moose never made up for their bad start in life, and most disappeared before their second birthday. Initially, I felt sad for these tiny moose with no future, but eventually Isle Royale taught me to love the big picture; there is beauty in the whole, including disease, bad weather, ticks, and tapeworms.

One of the best characteristics of my new job as Rolf's field assistant was the serendipitous nature of his research. While hiking cross-country, searching for dead moose and wolf sign, we found nests of osprey, goshawk, and bald eagle, new beaver ponds, glacial moraines, and relics of trapping and mining structures. Once we watched young red squirrels cautiously maneuver up and down the dead tree in which they had been born. The babies seemed just as terrified as I would have been, the first time or two; their agile, confident, acrobatic moves are learned.

Always particular about lunch spots, I insisted that we find a place with an interesting view and the proper mix of sunshine for me and shade for Rolf. In one such place we watched a beaver approach a moose feeding in a shallow beaver pond. Taking advantage of the long periods when the bull's head was submerged, the beaver glided to within three feet. Suddenly the glassy water was shattered by the sharp crack of the beaver's tail. Water exploded in all directions as the moose wildly splashed its way out of the pond and out of sight.

Rolf live-trapped red squirrels in the cedar swamp behind the cabin for a couple of summers to update research done by one of his predecessors and to determine the food base for pine marten, which the NPS considered re-introducing. This involved setting out one hundred traps baited with a mixture of peanut butter and oatmeal. News of a free lunch program travels fast, and the family of gray jays that patrolled the area quickly discovered that the benefits of getting caught outweighed the penalties of brief captivity and a compulsory plastic ankle-bracelet, a standard bird-banding device. Sometimes a bird entered another trap within ten seconds of its release from the first one. The red squirrels were not nearly as mellow as the gray jays. "It's as easy as handling a bolt of lightning!" commented Rolf's assistant Jim Woolington.

Fieldwork always necessitated field notes, a tradition Dr. Allen required, and much of our time at the cabin was spent filling out moose autopsy cards and drawing dots and lines on maps to record kill sites and hiking routes. Technology was crude in 1971, especially since we had no electricity. My sister visited us each summer and eagerly contributed to all our projects, including record-keeping. One very late night, she and I were calculating mortality rates for cows and bulls from various causes. I read the data off the autopsy card, something like, "cow, malnutrition," and she made a tally mark in one of ten columns on her paper. This was a major project, because mortality data had been collected for more than one thousand moose by 1974, and we were making good progress when I lost my place and asked, "What was the last one I told you?" Looking at a page full of tallies, she had no way of knowing which mark was last recorded. We had a good laugh at ourselves and started over again!

Rolf extended his field season as his class schedule at Purdue allowed, and we were fortunate to see the island in the fall. September and October have a characteristic nip to the air, as well as the peculiar odors of fungi and decomposing leaves. Squashberry (*Viburnum edule*) is a particularly smelly plant that grows in wet areas. Fall colors move, within just a few days, from the trees overhead to blanket the ground underfoot; soon the bright reds, oranges, and golds fade and darken, giving their energy back to the earth. The sun does not climb very high in the sky and gives noticeably less heat. Migrating snow buntings, white-crowned sparrows, juncos, horned larks, and Lapland longspurs foretell the season to come. The clouds are often low and gray, pushed by a northwest wind strong enough to lift our linoleum floor covering, even with the door closed, and whisk our oil stove's heat out the back wall. The furious storms of late fall remind us of our limitations, and we respect any creature with the fur, feathers, or ingenuity to survive.

Another boating misadventure occurred in the fall of 1974 when the "Wolf's" successor, a nineteen-foot Alumacraft with a 115-hp motor, sank right before our eyes. Our short dock necessitated tying the boat with the stern out, and during a storm in the middle of the night, large swells swamped it. Despite heroic bailing, we couldn't prevent the motor from being submerged by those angry rollers. When day broke, we radioed park headquarters, and the maintenance crew towed the sad boat to Mott Island, where they saved the motor, to our great relief.

The best way to keep warm in fall was to hike, but the limited daylight was a handicap. One morning in October 1974, we started from Moskey Basin and explored the rocky ridges and beaver ponds south of Intermediate Lake. About four o'clock in the afternoon, we came upon a freshly killed bull with a large rack of antlers, a rare find. Rolf skinned the metatarsus, which I stuffed, with jaws and pelvis, into my pack while Rolf shouldered the antlered skull. It was dark when we reached the park trail south of Lake Richie, pitch dark when we started the final two-mile leg to Moskey Basin. We knew the trail well, and all was fine until the East Pack of thirteen wolves tuned up nearby. It was a lovely group howl, not the eerie lone call that always sends shivers down my back; even so, I wondered whether the wolves could detect us amid all the tasty moose smells we were carrying. I found it reassuring to sing some rousing camp songs as we felt our way along the trail. We returned home exhausted and hungry and found a stick wedged in our door latch, Pete Edisen's welcome signal for, "The beans are hot, come on over."

We had little trouble with bulls during the rut, perhaps because of good fortune or the fact that both bulls and cows are preoccupied with each other for a few weeks. Moose are normally quiet animals, but they fill the chilly autumn nights with their grunts and moans in their determination to find one another. Rutting moose are unpredictable and deserve to be left alone to their mating traditions. A bull seems to regard every moving object as either a rival or a potential mate, so we purposely advertised our humanness when hiking in autumn. Several times we made large detours, deferring to bulls that obviously had no intention of yielding the path to us. Eating breakfast on our first wedding anniversary, we were surprised by two distracted bulls that ran right through our campsite. There was no time to climb a tree; we just froze. The bulls probably never even saw us!

One October we had a fantastic view of bulls sparring. Seated on the roof of the old Civilian Conservation Corps building at Siskiwit Bay, we watched three bulls size up each other. In the large clearing, the bulls were able to display their racks, slowly waving their massive heads and swollen "bells" from side to side. One bull was obviously smaller than the other two and quickly withdrew to the edge of the trees. The other two were about equal in size; after walking through the woods all summer, they knew just how big their antlers were. Slowly they approached each other, lowered their heads and carefully, almost gently, meshed their racks. Pushing with all their strength, each tried to force the other across some imaginary line. It didn't take more than ten minutes for one to claim the day, and the loser simply walked off the field. This was a fair fight, but not all are. We have found quite a large number of skulls with polished antlers, indicating the bull died between September and December, many more than with velvet-covered antlers, the condition of bull moose between May and September. It seems that the rut is a dangerous time for prime bulls. Simply a parting shot, a little poke in the paunch with those sharp points, can introduce fatal infection. Distracted and focused on each other, they may also be more vulnerable to wolves. Certainly they are noisier than at any other time of year, and wolves attracted to the grunts can also expect to find cows and calves nearby. Even without injury, big bulls face the storms of November in an exhausted state and may die before spring.

In those years as Rolf's assistant, I learned to live with mice, moose hair, and other specimens in our propane refrigerator. My college degree wasn't much help for the challenges I faced as Rolf's wife, field assistant, and camp cook. I remember receiving a questionnaire from the alumnae office, a follow-up of graduates, asking me to specify courses I found most helpful for my current work. Ha! We had just collected hundreds of wolf scats from an abandoned den site; should I mention Art History 215 or Economics 430? Now, there were new teachers: the wolves, moose, garter snakes, sore muscles, Lake Superior, rainbows, and the Edisens. I respected Rolf's meticulous methods and his patient commitment to accuracy. Earlier, I had wanted to understand everything, but gradually I learned to celebrate the complex, the unknowable.

As a young person on canoe trips, lying under a clear sky, night sounds in my ears, my eyes dazzled by an August meteor shower, I had had many opportunities to feel nature's power and beauty. I had always loved the Native American explanations for natural phenomena I had learned in Longfellow's *Hiawatha*, such as rainbows (heaven for flowers) and northern lights (death dance of warriors). It had seemed to me then that scientific explanations diminished my awe by leaving me in a fog of big words and difficult concepts. Now I realized that a scientist's joy of discovery is akin to the reverent perspective of the ancients; humility is common to both viewpoints.

As I trudged along behind Rolf mile after mile, our thoughts diverged. While he pondered something like the relationship between this year's crop of fir cones and last summer's drought, I wondered how far behind I could get in the six-foot-high thimbleberry plants before he would notice that I was missing, or why deer flies are more plentiful off trails than on, or how a business can get away with selling leaky rainsuits. I taught myself some new skills, such as how to take off a jacket without removing my backpack and the safest distance to allow when following Rolf through a dense spruce forest to protect my eyes from a rebounding branch. I made up new words to familiar melodies. Since Rolf did all the navigating, my mind was free to ramble.

I wondered what moose think of people, especially us "back to nature" types that need thirty pounds of gear to spend just a few days in the woods. The older moose, perhaps fifteen to twenty years old, have probably noted trends in tent styles and patterns on boot soles. June through August must seem to them the season of a large, noisy, but harmless and predictable pest.

And why do healthy moose not run from wolves but stand their ground or even charge at wolves? (This behavior makes it relatively easy for human hunters, using dogs, to kill moose: the dog confronts the moose, the moose makes its stand, and the human launches a spear, arrow, or bullet.) For some reason, a moose with problems like cysts in its lungs, arthritis, or weakness from malnutrition runs from danger, a behavior that triggers an impulse in wolves to chase. Why haven't moose learned to bluff, to feign health and strength, rather than run, a choice sometimes ending in death? I know that animals are capable of deceit when protecting their young. Perhaps good health cannot be faked. Often there is an odor to illness, as in an abscessed tooth, that even we can discern, so surely moose cannot hide this from wolves. Or perhaps moose simply know when it is time to die.

Yet, in winter 1977, Rolf and Don Murray watched a moose far out on the ice of Malone Bay, which is unusual because moose tend to avoid ice as it is slippery and offers no cover. The moose tracks ran in circles, and when Rolf and Don landed and got a closer look, they could see that its eyes were white. The bull was blind and was walking in circles to try to find shore. Along the shore, less than five miles away, came the East Pack of eleven wolves. It was getting dark so the plane had to return to camp, but tracks the next day showed that that old blind moose had fended off the wolves. The same pattern recurred the next night, and eventually the old bull walked into the icy water and drowned.

I also thought about hungry wolves and wondered why they don't just sample a human every now and then. People would be so much easier to catch and kill than moose. It seems our bad reputation is deeply entrenched, and wolf parents, raising their pups in seclusion, continue to tell the fearful stories of their heritage. And, though something in me would like to befriend a wolf, I know that, for their sake, I should keep my distance, allowing wolves to continue to regard people as their ultimate enemy. People and wolves have shared Isle Royale for sixty years, partly because people have respected wolves' need for space. We now have an improved attitude toward wolves, but it is best that they retain their low opinion of us.

As I came to know Isle Royale, I learned to respect the hardship inherent in nature. A wolf must catch and kill an animal whose skill at evasion has been evolving as long as the wolf's predatory skills, and it risks its life every time it tackles a moose, which can kick ferociously. A moose has problems of its own — processing forty pounds of leaves and twigs a day is hard on the teeth, and broken bones and injured joints cannot be set or replaced. Yet the hardships are what make the whole system spare and healthy, even beautiful to an outside observer. And, completely engaged in the present and not aspiring to live forever, wild animals seem content, unencumbered by guilt about the past, envy in the present, or worry about the future. The whole system is without malice. Wolves attack out of need, not anger, and in so doing perform their role in the scheme of things by protecting the trees that the moose need to live. I suspect those moose that died with incredibly arthritic joints or abscessed teeth did not resist their "annual physical" (Durward Allen's words). When wolves find a moose with a debilitating condition, the moose does not have an opportunity to leave the examination table to seek a second opinion. We, unaware and/or uncertain of our role in nature, are whiners and worrywarts, forever devising methods to avoid hardship, alleviate pain, and prolong life, cursing bad fortune, ungrateful for blessings. Unwilling to confront death's inevitability and our constant vulnerability, we invest in security measures that can actually increase our fears. Our culture of materialism and control enslaves us and robs us of our faith and our sense of well-being; I am careful whom I call a "dumb animal."

Although we were outside civilization's safety net (when we made navigational mistakes, misjudged the gap in a beaver dam, or forgot some piece of equipment, we suffered the consequences), Rolf and I had no delusions about independence. We relied on ripstop nylon tents, no-see-um-proof netting, white-gas stoves, raingear, compasses, and processed food. Beyond sophisticated camping gear, we needed others for financial and logistical support. Our groceries, garbage service, mail, telephone communications, and boat storage and maintenance came to us through the NPS, and we often hitch-hiked on park transportation from one end of the island to the other. We were grateful to be part of the human race, beneficiaries of inventions and goodwill.

We encountered people on Isle Royale in limited doses. Bangsund Cabin is situated a couple of miles by boat from park headquarters; we would make poor neighbors because of the bad-smelling moose bones often stewing in a pot in our yard. Even though isolated, both at the cabin and in the field, we had many opportunities to talk with visitors, and we soon realized that Isle Royale attracts an unusual sort of person. It is inconvenient and expensive to get to the island, and people do not arrive because they missed a turn in the road or want to impress people on their Christmas card list. Whether they come for fishing, scuba diving, backpacking, or sightseeing, visitors tend to be well informed and prepared to put up with the weather, insects, and inconvenience in order to absorb the subtle goodness of the island. Isle Royale helps people shed their veneer, exposing the good stuff underneath.

Our wonderful neighbors, Pete and Laura Edisen, told us about the early part of the twentieth century on Isle Royale, the era of commercial fishing, logging, Civilian Conservation Corps camps, resorts, and private homes. Earlier still, the island was burned and exploited by copper miners, whose stories are rarely told. Pete had lived on the island when the caribou disappeared, in the late 1920s. Working as a guide for early Biological Survey crews, he had seen the build-up and die-off of moose in the 1930s. He also watched moose, in confusion and panic, walk directly into the flames of the huge fire of 1936. Pete had seen some of the last coyotes, before they were killed off by wolves that arrived in the late 1940s. By Pete's account, red foxes fared well after coyotes were eliminated. Not only were wolves less able to kill foxes, they also began to provide moose carcasses for scavengers.

Laura was usually busy in the kitchen, serving up goodies to go with her grounds-in-the-pot coffee, but I remember one of her little adventures. For a few years, her brother Milford's family lived at the Rock Harbor Lighthouse, a quarter-mile from the Edisen cabin. One dark night, Laura went to deliver something to Milford in a tin pail. As she walked the path in the pitch black, she suddenly sensed that there was something directly ahead of her. She stopped and slowly stretched out her arm until . . . uff da! A moose! She turned and ran, and Pete remembered hearing that pail clatter all the way home. Laura had no idea what the moose did.

The Edisen Fishery was a living history exhibit — Pete set nets often enough to keep the place smelling fishy. He told visitors about the good and bad times for a commercial fisherman on Lake Superior, and everyone could see that subsistence living and inherent risk can bring out the best in a person. Pete loved chatting with visitors, but

26

it bothered Laura at times to be living in a "fish bowl" with people peering through their windows day and night. This was her present life, not quaint history, and she was disappointed that the park's long-range plan to fix up the cabin allowed the place to fall apart while she and Pete were living there. One day some scuba divers discovered an old frying pan in fifteen feet of water off the fish house dock. I guess they figured Laura had accidentally dropped the pan and would be pleased with its retrieval, but they got a surprise: "I burned everything I fried in that pan," Laura called out from her doorstep, "and I threw it in the lake because I never wanted to see it again!"

Laura's last summer was 1974, a miserable one for her and Pete. She was ill, but she had never consulted a doctor and wasn't about to break that seventy-five-year-old tradition. I regret that I encouraged her to seek medical help; we all thought she had diabetes. Laura knew, when she finally flew to a hospital in Two Harbors, Minnesota, that she would never return to Isle Royale. The diagnosis was pancreatic cancer, and she died in less than a month.

Dear Pete was never the same. The breakup of the partnership that had worked so well for so long was irreparable. Laura had done all the cooking and bookkeeping, and Pete, at seventy-eight, had trouble with both. He came to the island from his winter home in Two Harbors for three more summers, but they were difficult. I remember him, sitting on the fish house dock, with a battery-operated record player, listening to the "Blue Skirt Waltz." "We used to dance to it, Laura and I," he said tearfully. Pete died in 1982, but he and Laura live on in our memories — Pete with his tireless good humor and patience, Laura for her generous, Scandinavian style coffee and her additions and corrections to Pete's stories. From them I learned about goodness: that simple, radiant aura that most of us keep hidden from view. The Edisens continue to inspire those of us who knew them, encouraging us to rethink the meaning of success. They embodied a piece of Dag Hammarskjöld's wisdom:

> If only I may grow:
>   firmer, simpler
>   quieter, warmer. (p. 93)

Part Two: 1980s
Motherhood — Teaching

Rolf and I continued to migrate between Isle Royale and Indiana. By 1973 we were "hooked" on the island and wondered how we could ever leave. Its size is perfect — small enough to become familiar, yet large enough to pique one's curiosity year after year as weather, plants, and animals alter the landscape. Rolf finished his PhD in 1974 and was pleased to stay on the project for a post-doctoral year. At the end of that year, Dr. Allen retired, handing the reins to Rolf, who was greatly honored by his trust.

We wanted to be closer to the island, however, and sought a new winter home for the project. Houghton, Michigan, site of the park headquarters and Michigan Technological University (MTU), was eminently appropriate. Rolf signed on as an Assistant Professor of Biological Sciences at MTU, and we moved in the spring of 1975, renting another U-Haul. This time our cargo was much greater; we were hauling the eighteen-year collection of moose bones. We entered the real world that year, buying our first car and our first, and only, house. Still bigger changes lay ahead.

During the next winter study, Dave Mech flew to Isle Royale and tempted Rolf with an offer of work in Alaska, a wildlife biologist's dream. The Kenai Peninsula, southwest of Anchorage, had wolves and moose to be studied, and Rolf seemed the best man to do the job. My reaction to Dave's proposal was unequivocal and strong: I sobbed myself to sleep for several nights. Things had seemed so perfect, both on Isle Royale and in Houghton; why risk it all? I was thankful that Rolf felt a strong attachment to Isle Royale and loyalty to Durward Allen. He negotiated an arrangement with the university and the U.S. Fish and Wildlife Service whereby we would go to Kenai for three years, though he would return each winter to Isle Royale for the winter study. Rolf seemed confident that this temporary move would be good for Isle Royale and for our marriage; I trusted him and dried my tears.

At twenty-eight years of age, I confronted that important question: what about having a family? I asked Mom why she and Daddy had decided to have children, but her answer, "If you have to ask that, we must have failed," made no sense to me at the time. We were content as a couple and knew the powerful ecological arguments for having no children, but I simply, selfishly perhaps, wanted this chapter in life's adventure. Also, I knew Rolf would make a terrific father. Alaska suddenly seemed a fine spot to have a baby.

We left Isle Royale in the best of hands. Our competent summer assistant, Joe Scheidler, agreed to supervise the summer field season. For the next three summers, the tradition of thorough coverage of the island was maintained by Joe, his wife Lee, and their two assistants.

We arrived in Kenai in July 1976, taking another fine Isle Royale assistant, Jim Woolington, with us, and Rolf and Jim spent the rest of the summer getting to know the study area, many times bigger than Isle Royale and home not only to wolves and moose but also brown bear, black bear, caribou, and coyote. A four-wheel-drive truck replaced hiking boots, and Rolf and Jim mastered the techniques of trapping and telemetry. It was all I could do to learn the names of landmarks on trap lines; getting a feel for the place would take more time than I had, for our first child would be born in January.

I bounced around in the research truck on those rugged roads until September, then began a temporary job as a tutor at Soldotna Junior High School. This was my first teaching job, and while it was satisfying to help one twelve-year-old boy learn to read, the authors of *Old Yeller* and *Where the Red Fern Grows* did most of the work. I felt overpaid and underutilized; motherhood would provide a lesson in contrasts!

Jeremy David Peterson greeted the world on January 7, 1977, the second baby of the year in Soldotna's tiny hospital, where five moose browsed outside my window. Rolf was with me, having given up his seat in the research plane, a real sacrifice since he missed a rare sighting of wolves killing a moose. But holding a newborn is one of life's ecstasies, a moment for parents to share.

I was surprised at the strength of the maternal bond that developed over the first weeks of Jeremy's life — never meddle with a cow and calf! Nevertheless, twenty-nine-year habits of independence are hard to break, and one morning I found myself halfway to the grocery store before I realized I had forgotten my child at home, asleep. But being an older mother had some advantages. As a couple, we were well prepared in many ways to accept responsibility for a new life. And having no profession, I could willingly and joyfully relinquish a big chunk of my freedom.

However, when Jeremy was just two weeks old and I was on the verge of exhaustion, Rolf headed south to winter study on Isle Royale. My confidence was at a low ebb and I felt terribly vulnerable. To help me through those dark winter days, Mom flew to Kenai for a two-week visit. I don't know whether her lack of knowledge of diaper-folding and bath-giving was real or feigned, but it was the perfect medicine for my insecurity. I had spent the whole pregnancy preparing for labor and knew very little about baby care. Mom's endorsement of things I was doing shored up my wobbly self-esteem. It was also good to learn that babies are resilient and blessed with short memories, since I made lots of mistakes.

Because Rolf's work consumed much more than forty hours per week, it was obvious that I would give the quantities of time parenting requires. However, his calm, positive influence was vitally important to me, and I appreciated his support, both moral and monetary. Rolf told me that bringing home the bacon gave purpose to the hardest days at work, and he never suggested I earn supplementary income. Neither of us desired the lifestyle that would require me to work for money.

I found motherhood to be fascinating and fun, its responsibility awesome, its creativity unbounded. In retrospect, I wish I had shared Jeremy with more people, but I was a product of our culture of individualism and held tightly to the reins. Since we had decided to encumber the world with a child who would inevitably consume a disproportionate share of Earth's resources, we wanted to raise a responsible person, and that would take time, love, faith (and luck). It was wonderful to reread favorite children's books and discover new ones, to go for slow walks, to take Jeremy to church, and to remember the joy of small and simple things. We lived out of town and Jeremy learned to entertain himself. He was so good at it that I was able to begin a new hobby, quilting, which prompted Jeremy's first sentence: "Mommy, no sew!"

We spent two-and-a-half years in spectacularly beautiful Alaska. I often wondered how we would ever return to the Midwest. We lived in our dream house, creatively built by the first refuge manager and his wife, Dave and Eloise Spencer, with a root cellar, warming oven in the chimney, drawers built into the risers of the open stairway, and interior "window boxes" for plants and lichens. The house stood on 125 acres of land, complete with a creek in which king salmon spawned. The garden produced huge vegetables in record time, almost like the giant ones you see on postcards. Since our sojourn was to be temporary, we traveled as much as possible, frequenting Denali National Park, famous for its broad vistas and wildlife shows. The friendships we made in Alaska were strong and filled the gap created by distance from families "outside."

In some ways, however, Alaska made me nervous—such a treasure in the hands of technophiles! Because of the oil boom, people could afford to penetrate remote areas with vehicles and weapons to carve out private estates; machismo was alive and well. The place brings out the competitive juices in a person. I was appalled at myself, standing shoulder-to-shoulder with other fishermen, infected by the lust for salmon! More access roads were demanded, and on radio talk shows people like us, newly arrived from Oklahoma, Texas, or Michigan, suggested that "outsiders" no longer be allowed into the state.

Another problem for me was Alaska's magnitude. Isle Royale had taught me the value of familiarity with a natural area; Alaska's vastness was inspiring but unknowable, and my tourist activity damaged fragile landscape. And, of course, there were bears in Alaska. Doug Smith, one of our favorite Isle Royale assistants and now the director of the wolf project in Yellowstone National Park, told me that vulnerability is an essential element in his wilderness experience. Doug was far wiser than I—with a baby in my backpack I was reluctant to become part of the food chain. Besides, whenever bears and humans tangle, bears ultimately lose. I am willing to give them exclusive rights to some territory.

We returned to Isle Royale in 1979 with two-year-old Jeremy, eager for new adventures. Nature had been hard at work in our absence, and Rolf's winter counts showed that the moose population had been cut in half in the late 1970s. The wolves had built up to record numbers and were putting a lot of pressure on the remaining moose, especially calves. Whereas in the past wolves had not been able to affect an increasing moose population, they could prolong its low point and thus help the forest recover. Stands of balsam fir, decimated by moose ten years before, were now given a reprieve.

With moose numbers down, it was inevitable that wolves would decline, but Rolf was surprised to see it happen so quickly. From a peak of fifty in 1980, they fell to fourteen by 1982. Because of the "hands-off" nature of his research, Rolf was not able to take blood samples from the wolves and thus could not be sure of the reasons for the decline. Food shortage was a likely factor. Those old, vulnerable moose were gone, and the few remaining ones were thriving in the rebounding forest. Compared to the scrawny specimens we had seen in the early 1970s, young moose now seemed huge, certainly strong enough to fend off wolves. In desperation, wolf packs traveled outside their own territories to find food, and several were killed in interpack battles.

During summers in the early 1980s, our team found five dead wolves. A couple of them were nothing but skin and bones. These were the first complete wolf carcasses I had ever seen, and I was amazed at the story of hardship recorded in their bones. Cracked scapulae, jaws, skulls, ribs—no wonder only the most experienced wolves attack moose, with pups and others serving as cheerleaders. Commonly, injuries were old and healed; starvation had dealt the final blow.

In addition to a shortage of food, disease was a possible cause of the wolf crash of 1980–82. Canine parvovirus, a particularly virulent bug, ran rampant through the Upper Peninsula of Michigan at that time. Even though dogs are not permitted on Isle Royale, parvovirus could have come to the island on the soles of hikers' boots or through some other means. The disease would have been particularly hard on pups, and, indeed, Rolf saw no pups in winter 1982, a first.

For Rolf, not knowing the precise cause of the wolf decline was a major disappointment, and, in hindsight, he wished he had taken samples of some wolves' blood for testing. He began the effort necessary to get NPS permission to handle the Isle Royale wolves for the first time.

The traditional, observational winter study continued in much the same way as it had since 1959, except for a change in pilots. Don Murray's retirement in 1979 was painful for Rolf. But a friend of Don Murray, Don Glaser, of Alaska, took over and has faithfully served the Isle Royale project ever since. Besides being a skillful pilot, he has spiced up the winter study scene with his unique, lively sense of humor. A dull moment is a rare opportunity for Don, a specialist in practical jokes, particularly at mealtimes. One learns quickly to monitor one's plate and utensils.

Winter study continued to mark the low point of my year, coinciding with post-Christmas doldrums. Having a child brightened some days but lengthened others. The hurdle I had to get over each year was my dependency on Rolf. Friends helped immeasurably, as did church activities, winter picnics in the yard, story hour at the public library, and a weekly neighborhood coffee party. The island itself, frozen in ice but ready to come to life again in spring, gave me courage by raising my sights and broadening my perspective, helping me deal with my vulnerability.

I was always eager for Rolf's winter news, and on one occasion his research findings helped me directly. While in Alaska I had become a certified childbirth educator, teaching Lamaze relaxation techniques to help women cope with the pain of labor. Rolf told me about a wounded cow moose who calmly chewed her cud while wolves fed on her hindquarters. The cow seemed to feel no pain. The scientific explanation is that endorphins, chemicals released into the bloodstream during times of extreme stress, act like morphine. Researchers have found that endorphin levels in pregnant women increase just before labor begins. While I didn't want my students to equate giving birth with being eaten by wolves, I could encourage their faith in natural processes.

Beginning in summer 1979, I came to Isle Royale as a mother instead of a research assistant, and I was concerned that I would be frustrated by constraints on my time and activity. How I had loved the exploration and adventure of those early years! It was difficult, at first, to forego the hiking, but introducing new summer assistants to the island, making sure they had the best possible food and equipment while in the field, and spoiling them with homemade bread and pies when they returned gave me a new way to contribute. Once again, a dreaded change turned out to have some major advantages.

The movement to and from Isle Royale each summer became more complicated with a child, but we never considered staying in town. Rolf's research was central to our family's existence, and my help still seemed important. Also, the island was always my recharging station, restoring my faith and optimism. The disruption of moving made me take stock, closing accounts left behind and establishing goals for the season ahead. After a few minutes at Bangsund Cabin, with smells of balsam fir and cedar and sounds of spring peepers, kinglets, and loons, I was perfectly happy to be on the island.

Initially I wondered if it was right to raise a toddler in isolation from his peers, but Jeremy was obviously happy in the company of wild things and Lake Superior. During our engagement, Rolf had given me Rachel Carson's book *The Sense of Wonder*, and this provocative gem (reissued in 1998 by HarperCollins) now guided me. Jeremy's inborn sense of wonder needed little nurturing. Taking Carson's advice, we did not insist that he learn names of flowers and birds; we simply gave him the chance to explore and look closely. Perched on the shore of an aroused lake whose gray, frothy waves pounded the rocks at our feet, Jeremy nestled into my lap, entranced and respectful. Lake Superior, a dominant force in Isle Royale's climate, has always been tangled up with my religion, and I wanted Jeremy to feel its power and know his place. Few human errands are important enough to challenge this inland sea when it kicks up its heels.

Years before, I had found beauty at the edge of an Isle Royale beaver pond. Jeremy taught me to focus even closer to home. Like all young children, he taught his parents to slow down, to play "Poohsticks" in water flowing beneath trail boardwalks, and to celebrate variety in stones on the beach. One morning Jeremy announced he heard a blue and white sparrow singing outside his window; his joy was not diminished because he did not know the bird's proper name, nor was ours. Much has been written about a parent's gift to a child. The heart-warming laughter and refreshing perspective children give to adults should be put into the balance. All too easily, our vision and hearing become dull, we notice problems rather than promise, and let our pride supplant our praise.

My most difficult summer was 1980, a benchmark by which later years were measured. Our second son, Trevor, was just two weeks old when we went to the island, and he was not the easy baby Jeremy had been. Content only when carried, he made me walk miles inside Bangsund Cabin that summer. Even when half asleep, Trevor knew when I sat down in the rocking chair and would express his displeasure.

And Jeremy, the sunny three-year-old in whom I had seen great potential, now seemed destined for a career behind bars. With Trevor so obviously helpless and miserable, Jeremy could understand that the poor baby was blameless, and since Mom and Dad had caused the problem, they would pay the penalty. I tried to teach Jeremy to recognize the voices of temptation and conscience with which we all deal. Something sank in: one morning, as I made the bed with Jeremy riding on the brass frame, he said he was climbing Mt. St. Helens, which had erupted the day of Trevor's baptism. When I told him to be careful because the volcano was still rumbling, he remarked confidently, "Don't worry, Mommy, Mt. St. Helens has a conscience!" In a rare quiet moment Jeremy summed up his difficulties: "Mommy, what I really wanted was a big brother."

"Why did we ever think we could be decent parents?" That summer's diary is full of such entries. Rolf coped by using a combination of earplugs and earmuffs, and we put in many late nights, typing and pacing. Hikes in 1980 were rare. When Rolf was in the field, I found it difficult to make a trip to the outhouse, let alone step outside with my binoculars to identify a bird whose unfamiliar song tantalized me. I did our laundry by hand and washed cloth diapers in a metal tub over a fire. My admiration for Mrs. Bangsund skyrocketed, for she had raised three children in this cabin. And finally, we worried about our tenuous financial situation at the university, where Rolf's salary came from "soft money," outside grants that needed annual renewals.

One good thing about that summer was our superb field crew, Doug Smith and Mark Cramer, and I lived vicariously off their adventures. When they saw wolves frolicking in pools above a little waterfall, I was only a little bit jealous. Although we had different tasks to perform, we were still a team, looking outward together.

After one hard summer with a fussy newborn, Isle Royale became a wonderful place to raise children. Awakened by gray jays, warmed by sunshine, entertained by a beach with an unlimited supply of stones to throw, lulled to sleep by loons, the children found life enchanting, both outside and inside. We replaced worn linoleum, but there was still no way to keep wildlife out of the cabin, so I rejoiced when my baby learned to walk, lessening his contact with the floor. Trevor outgrew his colic and became a delightful little boy, and Jeremy turned out to be a fantastic big brother. We were lucky to suffer no major illnesses or accidents. Once, Trevor got a bad cut on his hand from a broken bottle, but I, who had often fainted at the sight of blood, managed to tend his wound and calm his fears like a confident nurse, though I felt woozy afterwards. I worked out an efficient system of washing diapers and actually came to enjoy the sunny-day chore, except for hauling bucket upon bucket of water from the dock.

Constrained only by lifejackets, the boys thrived on the freedom the island allowed. A hefty rope with a knot at the end, tied to an overhanging cedar, old fishing floats and driftwood, and a dishpan in which to mix "morningtop," a magical concoction of mud, pine needles, and whatever else was in season, were far better toys than the plastic, battery-operated gadgets we left in town. The boys kept busy with their imaginings. I was glad they had each other, since I could not participate with honest enthusiasm in their creative games and bizarre motor noises.

Each summer the boys built boats, which progressed from old boards tied to strings, which could be pulled around the dock, to elaborate but stationary contraptions devised from treasures found in the park scrap heap at Mott Island. Jeremy outfitted one of his more sophisticated on-shore boats with a sail made from a garbage bag and pulleys. Trevor wanted to be allowed to use it, so he devised changeable scenery on a scroll arrangement for the portholes. Jeremy could roll in halcyon or hurricane and then call the weather report to Trevor in his junk craft nearby. Trevor's ultimate model could be converted from a boat to an airplane in seconds.

As the years passed, our boys' homemade contraptions actually floated. Jeremy's first, crafted from plans in *The American Boy's Handy Book*, resembled one of Pete Edisen's square net boxes. It was clunky but safe, and it served its major function well: a base for attachments such as "radar," "sonar," and "loran." Always on Jeremy's heels, Trevor soon launched his own rowboat. I relaxed when they were out on the water in two boats so one boy could rescue the other if there were a mishap.

One tradition I was determined to maintain, regardless of children, was blueberry picking in August. Blueberries grow in beautiful places and are ripe when most of the bugs are gone. A compulsive picker, I couldn't let a good berry year go by without spending several days in a patch. Although I did not expect the boys to be of much assistance, I intended to keep them amused long enough to be able to fill a few buckets. One year I pitched a tent and set the boys up with Matchbox cars and crayons and paper, but the novelty wore off in less than an hour. Another day Jeremy brought along his new toy bow and rubber-tipped arrows. Before I unpacked the berry buckets, Jeremy shot an arrow into the air — and in the course of our search for it he had a run-in with hornets. For me, it was just as well that the early 1980s did not produce bumper berry crops.

When the boys reached school age, both of them began taking violin lessons in town during the academic year. Jeremy expressed his interest in the violin as a five-year-old, and I signed him up with the Suzuki teacher. He had always been a good singer, and now he took an instant liking to the instrument, making rapid progress. It undoubtedly felt good to be able to do something that his parents couldn't do. Trevor, when five years old, asked for lessons, too, even though he had witnessed major mother-son squabbles during practice sessions. Since the boys could play by ear, there was no limit to their repertoire, and it was rather nice to be free from the regimen of scales and etudes in the summer.

Only one child could practice music at a time in our tiny cabin, so I assigned "school work" to the idle boy each morning. The cabin was a wonderful place to study. Once we declared recess to watch an otter catch and eat a herring less than ten feet from the window. The boys chose the topics — Latin, world history, literature — and when each was eleven years old, he wrote his autobiography. Most important, the morning regimen made everyone appreciate the rest of the day's freedom even more.

Reading was one of our joys, never a chore, and rainy days allowed us to become immersed in some of the great classics of our language. I read aloud while the boys worked on art projects. If summer assistants had paperwork to do, they joined the party, sometimes asking me to read their childhood favorites. One effect of shared reading was that the boys were on the same wavelength when they played, inspired by *The Adventures of Tom Sawyer*, *The Wind in the Willows*, and *Treasure Island*. Reading was a sacred, just-before-bedtime activity, and as the boys grew older and I spent too much time scolding, we all enjoyed focusing on someone else's adventures at the end of the day.

We never spent much time fishing. Perhaps we wasted a marvelous opportunity, but since there was often a commercial fisherman living next door, we bartered homemade orange rolls and lemon meringue pies for fresh trout, whitefish, and herring. Jeremy was our most persistent fisherman. One summer he fed worms to a brook trout under our dock, but in August, when he caught the fish, I think he felt he had betrayed a friend. In 1989 he was casting off our dock when two men in a skiff trolled past. "Any luck?" called one of the fishermen. "Oh, yes!" replied Jeremy cheerfully, "I got one four years ago!" The fishermen took pity and gave him a lovely three-pound lake trout. Trevor hasn't fished since he lost his lure to "a big one" which towed him in his boat quite a distance before breaking the line. He found it painful to think of that fish swimming around with a barbed hook in its mouth. He lost his innocence that day, realizing that his actions have consequences.

Rolf and I had the equipment, the wilderness, and the will to go camping, but the boys seemed uninterested. Backpacking is hard work, and the kids were content with their homemade boats and imaginative games. Our first major trip was in 1985, when we surveyed the island's nesting loon population. This was a canoe trip, however, and we could carry those "extras" that make camping pleasant. When backpacking, we found it best to make short outings with one child at a time. Three-year-olds are delightful company on overnight camp-outs, and for several years the wolves were near enough to the cabin so that a short hike enabled us to pitch our tent within ear-shot of their howling.

Jeremy had to be taught to love the sound of a wolf howl. As a two-year-old, he first experienced that eerie sound on a tape recording we had made, and it brought frightened tears. I could empathize with him. I had spent a night alone in a tent with wolves howling from opposite directions, and one wolf had trotted, panting, right past the tent. I lay there, grasping my Mini-Maglite, visualizing grisly contingencies. Even though my mind reassured me that wolves are not dangerous, something made me afraid. While camping, we taught Jeremy about wolf language, and he became as excited as we were to hear howling.

The greatest deterrents to enjoyable camping on Isle Royale are bugs and bad weather. We have been cold and wet for days, when our only dry things were food and sleeping bags. Black flies crawl up pant legs and sleeves and raise bloody welts behind one's ears. Mosquitoes can drive a person crazy with their persistent swarming and buzzing. My least-favorite pests are no-see-ums, whose bites hurt and then itch for hours. Deer flies circle our heads and backpacks as we walk in July and August. And stable (sand) flies, the scourge of canoeists and fishermen, specialize in biting ankles and seem impossible to swat.

The boys and I made a memorable overnight trip one August. Camped on a ridge overlooking a lake with a resident loon family, the boys watched a peachy full moon rise while I read Longfellow's *Hiawatha* aloud to them. The boys tended to like facts and science, but there are other ways to look at the moon.

The young men and women who assisted us each summer became important members of our family. Each time they returned from a trip, they shared their adventures; research was always the focus of our Isle Royale life. In 1981, we covered our kitchen table with a topographic map of the island, a practical and symbolic move. As soon as the boys could hike a bit, they were invited, one at a time, to go on overnight expeditions with the assistants. In July 1983, Edith Greene took Jeremy on one such overnight. I decided to camp in a different spot, which left Rolf at home with Trevor. The next morning Rolf met me on the dock with, "Tonight, I am going camping and you can stay here." A bat, which lived in our wall, had chosen to hunt mosquitoes inside the cabin, and Rolf had been up much of the night encouraging it to leave.

Each year the boys ventured a bit farther into their big backyard. To the northeast of the cabin there was a grave, surrounded by a weathered, lichen-covered picket fence. We had heard various stories as to who was beneath the sunken ground, and the consensus is that a group of miners, killed in a brawl over liquor, lie in the spot. Most of those hapless miners had been buried on nearby Cemetery Island. The boys had no qualms about the grave, and Jeremy and a pal even camped inside the fence one night.

Determined not to pass along my near-phobic attitudes about spiders and snakes to our children, I spent a lot of time watching these creatures. I learned how to remove garter snakes from behind cupboards and underneath Trevor's crib. The boys' fascination with all things furtive and slippery helped me develop tolerance; I am still working on fondness.

Now that we were staying close to the cabin, we got to know some long-time Isle Royale visitors. Stan and Margaret Van Antwerp were a colorful couple with an ambitious yet respectful approach to the island. They determined to explore all the inland lakes, which meant portaging their twelve-foot homemade canoe through swamps and over ridges without benefit of trails. They caught and ate pike wherever they went and supplemented fish with cattail shoots, berries, and other wilderness bounty. Margaret was particularly proud of their camping style, challenging anyone to find even one of their campsites, for they carefully perked up the vegetation after striking their tent each morning. Dutifully observant, they took careful notes when they saw moose, loons, beaver, or bones. We looked forward to their annual visit, toward the end of July, and counted on hearing their natural history observations.

Colonel "Tempe" and Betsy Cawthorne came each summer in their Carver boat, which they "anchored out," so they could stay beyond the two-week NPS dock limit. The Colonel was particularly enamored of the island's mining history and guided his own tours to the Minong Mine for any McCargoe Cove campers who were interested. Betsy especially loved orchids that thrive in Isle Royale's cool, damp climate. Crippled by arthritis and needing two canes to get around, she managed to lead me to a patch of showy lady-slippers that bloom every Fourth of July.

In 1984, I served as board chairman for the Isle Royale Natural

History Association, whose mission is to provide maps, books, and other information to Isle Royale visitors. In this capacity I was introduced to those few remaining families who held life leases to property in the park. These folks tended to stay close to their homes and did not get to know the island in the same way backpackers did, but their love for Isle Royale was just as strong as mine, and their experience and perspective just as valid.

Of course, there were some times when I would gladly have given my life at Bangsund Cabin to any taker. One night in the middle of August 1985, a rainy summer with Lake Superior at a high level, while Rolf was conferring with colleagues in Edmonton, Alberta, I did my best to hold our estate together through a rip-snorting thunderstorm. Fortunately, the boys were sound sleepers. The dock, somewhat anchored to the gravel shore with two three-foot sections of pipe, was bucking and pulling loose, so I moved the skiff, which was tied to a cleat on the dock, to the shore. I pulled it out of the water as best I could, but even with the bow nosed up to the cabin window, the surging waves pounded and rocked the boat until I piled rocks and logs in the bow, raising the stern above all but the highest thudding waves. I then found a rope and tied one end to the dock cleat and the other to the big cedar tree on shore. Meanwhile, our roof leaked steadily, and I had to keep an eye on coffee cans and dishpans that were set out to catch drips, making what Pete Edisen called Chinese music. That night I wrote in my diary, "There are times I hate this place—always when I am afraid."

Even though we respect Lake Superior and tend not to take chances, sudden winds and storms have surprised and tested us. The boys and I once over-stayed a wonderful party on Minong Island in Tobin Harbor. Rounding Scoville Point in our fourteen-foot skiff, I encountered heavy chop and large swells. Frightened, yet determined to appear calm for the children, I glued a smile on my face and sang a cheery sailing song, thinking all the while, "You fool! What are you doing out here?" (The boys were not duped by my acting and remember my stern voice telling them to sit on the floor of the boat.)

Another journal entry, made in 1982, reminds me that motherhood is an uneven career. Some days I felt anyone could do a better job of raising children than I was doing. I was the primary care-giver and disciplinarian and had to live with Jeremy's pronouncement: "Mommy brings the bad news." My mistakes taught me to apologize; I hope the boys learned to forgive. If nothing else, they learned to see another human being in all stages, sometimes singing and dancing around the kitchen, other times in a fury. I like to believe that it is our imperfections that make us lovable.

I hope, too, that our sons learned to cherish this Earth, and that the words of an old camp song, sung before breakfast at the shore of a quiet lake, will always speak to their souls:

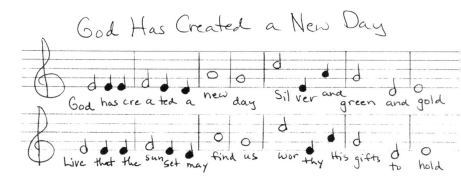

God Has Created a New Day

God has cre a ted a new day Sil ver and green and gold
Live that the sunset may find us wor thy His gifts to hold

Like all mothers, I became an expert juggler. Once I had been totally immersed in Rolf's field research, but now each day was a unique mixture of domestic and research chores, bread-making and bone-measuring, with weather determining the schedule. I enjoyed having my whole family together, united by the work so important to Rolf.

Jeremy and Trevor taught me to see the world through their innocent, honest vision. Trevor was about three years old when he spent a few days with my sister, the boys' beloved Aunt Deedee, at her cabin in the woods of northern Minnesota, and she told me they had watched a newly fledged red-breasted nuthatch sit on a stump and beg for food. Months later, out of the blue, Trevor asked, "Why did the peanut shell sit on a stump and cry for its mother?" I wracked my brain. Too young for riddles, Trevor was asking a serious question. Several days later I made the connection: peanut shell = nuthatch!

And one Christmas night in Houghton, as I tucked two-year-old Jeremy into bed, I asked him what he had liked best about Christmas. I was hoping he would recall the candlelight service at church that had brought tears to my eyes. Jeremy thought awhile, then answered pertly, "People giving me presents." Not really surprised, I explained that someday he would discover the joy of giving gifts. Again there was a long pause, then: "Will that be when I am old enough to use big scissors?"

I suffered two miscarriages after Jeremy was born, and I feared I could not provide him with a sibling. The second episode was particularly difficult because I was in the fourth month of pregnancy. As I lay on the living-room couch and cried, Jeremy, putting around the house in a little plastic car, asked me what was wrong. "I'm just down in the dumps right now," I replied, and he immediately put my words to music: "Mommy is down in the dumps; be back pretty soon, okay?" How close are joy and sorrow!

In his poem on children in *The Prophet*, Kahlil Gibran advises parents to "strive to be like [your children], but seek not to make them like you." In town one September, after attending his first football game, Trevor piped up from the back seat, "Why don't they play with two balls so they don't have to fight with each other?" A few years later, as Trevor's Cub Scout den mother supervising a relay race, I watched a group of eight-year-olds spontaneously arrange themselves into teams that would produce a tie.

A shortage of babysitters made it impossible for Rolf and me to hike together when our boys were young, and I realized that if I was going to do any exploring I would have to master navigation by compass and topo map. After a few mistakes, I gained confidence and sometimes discovered something of interest, such as a loon chick, a dead moose, or an abandoned, rusty coyote trap. I hiked slowly and had time to learn the ovenbird's exuberant flight song, sung in evenings over clearings. Alone in the woods, I was quiet, open to the magic of the place. I have rarely felt so close to God, so tuned in to "the force" that flows through creation, and it occurred to me that this was "the peace that passes all understanding" I had felt from time to time in church. Years earlier, on my knees, saying the words of the General Confession ("We have erred and strayed from Thy ways like lost sheep"), I had felt connected to people who, for hundreds of years, had made the same admission, and, kneeling between my near-perfect parents, I realized that I would never outgrow this human experience of blundering, confession, and forgiveness. Both in church and in the woods, I felt completely alive, accepted, "a part of the main," overwhelmed with joyful humility, and loved. What a revelation, to be able to see that Christianity is completely compatible with my love of nature! How many other ways have people experienced this sense of oneness, the power of the Spirit?

As a camp counselor, I had made a collection of wise sayings, and one by Karl Rahner comes to mind as I try to explain this indescribable feeling:

> In love, the gates of my soul spring open, allowing me to breathe a new air of freedom and forget my own petty self. In love, my whole being streams forth out of the rigid confines of narrowness and self-assertion which make me a prisoner of my own poverty and emptiness. (p. 17)

One consistent effect of my solo reveries was that I returned home content and eager to pick up whatever burden I had left behind; deep gratitude demands expression. With small children at my feet and Rolf's research project always in need of help, my duties were clear. Refreshed and restored, I was pleased to have purposeful work to do. Like Laura Edisen, I put my praise into action through everyday chores.

> *To preserve the silence within — amid all the noise. To remain open and quiet, a moist humus in the fertile darkness where the rain falls and the grain ripens — no matter how many tramp across the parade ground in whirling dust under an arid sky.*
>
> — Dag Hammarskjöld, p. 83

Part Three: 1990s
Listening (and Letting Go)

In the 1970s I became attached to Isle Royale, a place I have come to know and love more than any other place on the planet. In the next decade, our children stretched me in new ways, yet grounded me in this world more firmly than ever before. There were more lessons, however, and in the 1990s my ears were attuned to new voices, whose deep tones were in perfect harmony with those I had heard earlier, in church and nature. My spirit was challenged, and I am still learning which things I can let go and which connections are sustaining.

Rolf kept the Isle Royale wolf-moose project small; funds are always difficult to come by, Bangsund Cabin's table seats only six, and our research activity has an impact on the wilderness we love. Field techniques have changed somewhat, but the research effort is highly consistent, making year-to-year comparisons meaningful.

The Park Service gave Rolf permission in 1988 to handle a few of Isle Royale's wolves to determine the cause of their population crash in 1980–82. This meant live-trapping and taking blood samples in spring, a step I dreaded because of the risk to the wolves. Rolf had the same concern, but he could not tell whether disease or genetic problems were adversely affecting the wolves until blood samples were analyzed. Also, radio collars would save a lot of air time in winter when locating wolves from the study plane.

Fortunately, the trapping operation went smoothly. Rolf always had the assistance of a veterinarian in case of accidents. Canine parvovirus antibodies were found, confirming that this disease had come to Isle Royale. What's more, genetic screening showed that all trapped wolves had descended from one female who crossed the ice from Canada in the 1940s. If parvovirus cut the population down to a low level, inbreeding might well cause extinction.

Beginning in 1988 we carried radio receivers and antennae along with our "kill kits" (saw, knife, rubber gloves, and plastic bags) when we hiked. From radio signals we learned that wolves do not avoid humans as much as we had thought. One wolf hung around Daisy Farm, close enough to hear the park ranger's evening program. Another time, when Rolf was away at a conference, I was assigned to keep track of the East Pack by monitoring radio signals from Ojibway Tower. The boys were not interested in a hike, and at the ages of eight and eleven they could be trusted on their own for a couple of hours. From atop the tower roof I heard, in the direction from which I had just come, the loud signal of the male wolf who ranged the length of the island. I really expected I might see the fellow, his signal was so strong. As I hiked back down the trail, the beeps continued to come from the same direction. He's right in Daisy Farm Campground, I thought. But no . . . from the Daisy Farm dock the signal, now very loud, was coming from near our cabin across Rock Harbor. As I groped in my pack for my binoculars, I had a brief moment of panic. Our boys were playing on the beach, unaware, of course, of the nearby wolf; I was surprised by my momentary loss of faith.

Undoubtedly enticed by our fragrant bone rack and the carcass of a drowned moose not far down the shore, the collared wolf hung around behind Bangsund Cabin for several days. When our summer assistants returned from a trip, we used telemetry equipment to try to catch a glimpse of the wolf. He was close; we could even smell him. He led us in one direction and then, a few seconds later, "reappeared" directly behind us, but we never saw him. Stripped of technology, the human animal is a modest creature indeed! This wolf died in January 1991 — old, starved, and with the usual complement of broken bones. He is now mounted and looks unrealistically beautiful in the visitor center at Windigo.

The same year Rolf first handled some of the wolves, Earthwatch volunteers began to lend their physical and financial support to the summer project. Since Rolf and I were not contributing to the fieldwork as much as we had in our first years on the island, we needed some help. Earthwatch, a private non-profit organization based in Maynard, Massachusetts, matches paying volunteers with field research projects all over the world. I wondered who would pay to do what we do, but not only did volunteers come, they came in significant numbers. And, most importantly, they enjoyed themselves! From Australia, Italy, Israel, New York City, and Los Angeles, from age fifteen to seventy-four, they had little in common when they arrived except a love for wild places and a desire to contribute to a research project they deemed worthwhile. For a week they put their lives in the hands of a team leader, usually one of our summer assistants. The trips were often very difficult, and even though a common focus fostered team spirit, many Earthwatchers found it the most challenging week of their lives. One volunteer jested, "You should offer an alternative: pay double and skip the hike!" Two volunteers were quoted (though they told me they were joking) in their California newspaper as having survived "a hike in hell!" But rainbows, moose sightings, trail food, and storms knit individuals together. The generosity, self-denial, sensitivity, tolerance, and forgiveness practiced by these volunteers are a prescription for our planet's ills. Earthwatchers have a chance to live a bit like wolves in a pack, making personal sacrifices for the common good, a habit that has fallen into disuse in our culture. Even more so than a wolf pack, an Earthwatch group is democratic—everyone gets the same sized cup, and there is no pecking order. My spirits soar when I think of these fine people, living and working all over the world, making a positive difference.

As "expedition coordinator," I packed food and equipment for our Earthwatchers and rewarded them at the end of their trips with fresh food. In our first year, we were overly confident and accepted fifty-eight volunteers. Three teams of six people were in the field simultaneously, and three days after they left the island, another eighteen folks were ready to start. One stormy night there were twenty-six people eating dinner in our small cabin. By the end of August, I was exhausted and irritable; the next year we down-sized.

Between Earthwatch trips I needed some time to recover and prepare for the next group. Our Earthwatch leaders, often our summer assistants, had the same needs. Since I was chief cook and bottle washer for a "family" of seven, I was always on duty. At one point I aimed some sharp, hurtful words at one of our assistants. Then, feeling terrible, I retreated to the hill south of our cabin, where I sat and sobbed in shame and frustration. In the empty aftermath, the wind in the trees overhead and the lichen at my feet soothed my anguished heart and gently exposed my pride and selfishness. As my anger changed to remorse, my determination to explain my side of the story evaporated. Suddenly I felt not only free but also courageous enough to apologize. I learned that humble pie has a pleasant aftertaste.

Earthwatchers have made terrific field assistants. A group of strangers tends to be quiet, open to the island's lessons; a wilderness setting brings out the best in human nature by constantly reminding people of our place in creation's beauty. Also, among new faces a whiner or bully has a chance to change, to shed a bad reputation, to become the person he or she really wants to be. Good-natured banter is common on Earthwatch trips, and humor is arguably the most important contribution Earthwatchers make to this research project; a good laugh keeps a scientist's perspective healthy. We have been blessed with some loyal volunteers who return year after year. Mike Thomas came fourteen years in a row, and he met his wife Kim on one of his early adventures here. Ron Eckoff began in 1989, coming every other year until retirement allowed him to come more often, bringing friends and relatives. Volunteer Tim Pacey has become a team leader, and the project's dealings with life and death helped him accept the tragedy of his young son's passing.

While Earthwatch greatly expanded our family, our summer assistants became increasingly influential role models for Jeremy and Trevor. Rolf has always selected his help carefully, looking for honest, hard-working young men and women who enjoy being outside. Our mealtime conversations may not have pleased Emily Post, but they reflected our shared commitment to Isle Royale. Our capable assistants first served as aunts and uncles, then siblings, and, finally, friends to our boys. Doug Smith promised three-year-old Jeremy a trip to Lily Lake, and, true to his word, in 1991 he led Jeremy to all the "hot spots" at the west end of the island. At thirteen, Jeremy was almost able to keep up with six-feet-five Doug. Another wonderful assistant, Tim Laske, invited Jeremy on a canoe trip with him and his new wife. How many newlyweds have the heart to share a canoe trip with a fourteen-year-old?

Earthwatch jolted fifteen-year-old Jeremy forward in his development; when our scheduled Earthwatch leader became suddenly ill, we roused him from sleep and asked him to consider leading the trip. I will cherish forever Jeremy's humility when confronted with this responsibility; it was the first time in a couple of years he had admitted there might be something he couldn't do. He was very concerned about operating the white-gas stoves, and while the volunteers approached the island, a six-hour boat ride from

Michigan, he practiced lighting every stove in our cache. At the same time, he memorized bird songs, names of flowers, and the history of the island's moose and wolves. He was a good leader, and we had never been more proud of him.

The wolf decline in the early 1980s gave Rolf the impetus to tackle the writing of a summary of his years with the wolf-moose project. He wanted to explain the options open to the NPS, should the Isle Royale wolves disappear, and to encourage people to make their opinions known, because a decision about the future of wolves on Isle Royale should be made in consultation with the public owners of the park, particularly scientists. Rolf gently stated his own position: as long as there are moose on Isle Royale, there ought to be wolves.

But he got off to a slow start. I had been hounding him to write, but my nagging was totally ineffective. Then, alone at the cabin for a few days in 1994, I thought, "By gum, I'll write my own book," and for the next three days I sat at our table, completely absorbed and exhilarated as words appeared on the paper. When Rolf learned what I had been up to, he was afraid I had taken his good stories. As he read the first page, however, he chuckled, "I don't think we have a problem here." My project spurred him along, and he quickly finished his book, *The Wolves of Isle Royale: A Broken Balance*.

Like an artist who learns to notice light, color, and shape, I found that once I began writing, new ideas kept surfacing. Every hike, every book, every new person, had a lesson for me. In a discussion with Paul Hayden, an editor at Lake Superior Press, I had made a remark about hoping to change the world. "Why? Is anything wrong with it?" was his quick response, which stuck in my head for a long time. Since college, I had been certain that the world was full of problems, and I was eager to fix one or two. By focusing on problems, I was developing a furrowed brow and losing my joy, thinking of things I (and others) should be doing rather than praising and encouraging the goodness that envelops us abundantly, even now.

While working on my manuscript in 1994, I met Gendron Jensen, an artist-in-residence on Isle Royale who specializes in much-larger-than-life drawings of bones. On a buggy, rainy afternoon he spent more than three hours selecting a few specimens to take to his studio. Puzzled, I asked him just what he was looking for. "I am waiting for one of the skulls to speak to me," he matter-of-factly replied. I had found, lugged, cleaned, labeled, measured, and stored these bones, completely oblivious to the energy our new artist friend detected in each specimen. Those bones do not speak to me, but I have no doubt that Gendron can hear them. Scientific or artistic value—who is to say which is more important? Fortunately, a single bone can serve several purposes. And while Gendron's reverence for bones is foreign to me, I am in awe of his genuine and powerful experience. There is a glow about Gendron Jensen, a man whose sense of wonder is intact.

Once I was telling a group of visitors who had come to see the Bangsund Cabin bone collection about Gendron Jensen's ability to hear the language of bones. One gentleman took me aside and thanked me for telling Gendron's story. "My son is an artist, too," he explained. "Great!" I responded. "What does he draw?" "German washing machines," was his reply.

Beginning in 1994, I assisted with the park's breeding bird survey each June. At last, birds were the focus of a hike, and I could stop to identify various sounds without having to rush to some distant point with a heavy pack. Rolf and Trevor were among my patient recorders, getting up at five o'clock in the morning, taking notes, and swatting mosquitoes. Birds establish their territories by singing, and even though some birds imitate their neighbors' songs and some individuals do not sing "by the book," a systematic survey of songs can indicate trends in species abundance. I realize that birdsong has a serious purpose and is quite aggressive, but it is among my favorite music, even so.

WHITE THROATED
SPARROW

Years later I took an ornithology class at MTU and learned that birds have evolved in amazingly diverse ways in order to penetrate a wide range of habitats. A "bird brain" is a marvel of nature. (I must speak to my brother, who for years got a rise out of me by calling me "bird," short for "bird brain"!) A black-capped chickadee can remember a phenomenal number of seed-storage sites and actually grows an enlarged hippocampus, the part of the brain that houses spatial memory, as needed. When no longer useful, the hippocampus degenerates; a bird cannot afford to carry around extra weight. A green heron uses an old leaf or other bait to attract fish to its feeding site. The malleefowl male builds a compost heap in which the female lays her eggs, and he carefully monitors the temperature of the nest, removing material during the day and adding insulation at night. Flight itself is an engineering wonder, as are the methods birds use to navigate during their long migrations.

In 1995, just as Jeremy went off to college, Rolf took a three-month sabbatical in Yellowstone National Park to participate in the wolf restoration project. Trevor attended school in Gardiner, Montana, and I used the new perspective to decide what to do with the rest of my life. From our house at Mammoth Hot Springs, we looked up to mountains in all directions. We bought our few housewares at a church rummage sale and lived simply. Though far from Isle Royale, I felt connected to its humble goodness, just as I had when in Alaska. Working on a quilt in the afternoon sun, I listened to the silence. (Blaise Pascal: "All human evil comes from this, man's being unable to sit still in a room.") This was new, and I realized that my mind had become numb from constant stimulation. Full of other people's ideas, I had become complacent and passive, even cynical. But now, sitting quietly, I set my internal radio on "scan" and heard some amazing things. Manageable projects, not ideas for global change, came to mind, and I had the time to act on my intuition's nudges as well as on the lessons offered by new people in my path.

One afternoon, I felt the urge to write a letter and later found that my letter had arrived at a crucial time. It felt as though I and the Post Office had participated in a miracle; proper timing can make all the difference, rendering my actions effective instead of intrusive.

To help decorate his Yellowstone room, Trevor used this quote from *Markings*, by Dag Hammarskjöld:

> You are not the oil, you are not the air—merely the point of combustion, the flash-point where the light is born. You are merely the lens in the beam. You can only receive, give, and possess the light as a lens does. If you seek yourself, "your rights," you prevent the oil and the air from meeting

the flame, you rob the lens of its transparency. Sanctity—either to be the Light, or to be self-effaced in the Light, so that it may be born, self-effaced so that it may be focused or spread wider. (p. 155)

I thought of people who transmit light clearly, like Pete and Laura Edisen. As Isle Royale fishermen, they worked long hours at a job that was physically demanding, sometimes dangerous, and always financially risky. Valuable nets might be lost in a storm, and after a poor season Pete and Laura could not afford the boat ticket back to the mainland. Yet the Edisens never let desire for something "more" interfere with their happiness. Content with their blessings and completely engaged in life, they did not want the sort of lifestyle that is killing our planet. Twenty years after the Edisens taught me to see light through the cracks in Bangsund Cabin's walls, I came across these words by Leonard Cohen:

> Ring the bells that still can ring,
> Forget your perfect offering
> There is a crack in everything
> That's how the light gets in. — "Anthem"

My mother's father was another clear lens. I remember, even as a child, noticing his constant good humor, and as I grew up, I learned that his difficult experiences could have made a lesser person a bitter old man. His father had died when Grampy was twelve, his mother was poor, his wife was ill for much of their married life, and the Depression and medical bills consumed most of his hard-earned money. Nevertheless, for about forty years he produced a weekly family letter, a single typed page recounting the events of his week with unfailing good humor. He never complained; if things at home were difficult, he included an anecdote from the minister's sermon or a joke from the "I Love Lucy" TV show. Grampy's faith in a loving God produced his radiance; he looked outward for the Light and transmitted it clearly. My grandfather, like the Edisens, was rich á la Henry David Thoreau, "in proportion to the number of things he can afford to leave alone"(p. 74). Immune to the temptations of wealth and status, my heroes were generous and joyful, more interested in loving than in being loved.

Dorothy Bishop, a Yellowstone friend, loaned me one of her favorite books, *1000 Beautiful Things*, edited by Marjorie Barrows. I hand-copied page after page—prose and poetry of people like Amiel, Peter and Catherine Marshall, Norman Vincent Peale, Goethe, and Bryan Jeffery Leech. My mind steeped in beautiful thoughts, I awoke in the middle of the night with an image that seemed to knit all these beautiful ideas together in a circle that related various human experiences (see the diagram "Voices and Choices"). If I listen carefully, I can hear voices that try to influence me. When Jeremy had been three, I had suggested he try to distinguish these voices. As we age, I think the voices become more subtle. Some seem to arise from fear and a need to be in control, and when we act on them we are lured into dead ends. Alternatively, the voice of love pulls us around the circle.

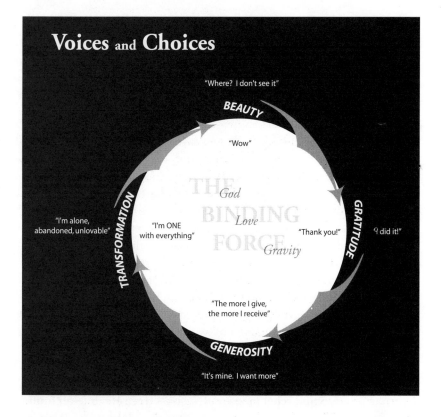

The Yellowstone sabbatical taught me to listen to the "music of the spheres," and to act on the impulses aroused by that music. Isle Royale is one of my favorite channels, but I am not always open to its messages. Experience has taught me to listen for similar messages on other stations. I believe all peak spiritual experiences, whether prompted by nature, religion, a new friend, small children, art, music, literature, meditation, science, tradition, hearty laughter, or a simple act of kindness, spring from the same source, producing a heavenly sense of well-being and connection. (These peaks show up as "beauty" on the circle.) The fact that we are not all tuned in to the same channel makes life interesting. I tend to be easily bored in an art gallery, but if I hear Tchaikovsky's "Fifth Symphony" while driving, I might be a road hazard! How sad that we sometimes try to impose our own mystical pathways on one another, as if there were only one way to know the power of the Spirit! And when we learn to celebrate diversity, not merely tolerate it, how much richer we will all be!

Refreshed and inspired by Yellowstone's grandeur, Rolf, Trevor, and I returned to Houghton in time for the 1996 winter, one that Pete Edisen would have called a "pea-doozer." I was jolted out of my sabbatical reverie as the winter began early, with violent storms, cold, and snow. When the thirty-eighth winter study opened in January, moose were obviously suffering. Wind-whipped shorelines had more exposed food for moose, but 2,500 animals had overbrowsed the fir, aspen, and mountain ash. Several moose reached too far for twigs and fell off cliffs. After mining their last fat reserves, stored in bone marrow, many moose, especially the calves and the old, starved. Rolf spotted sixty dead moose during his seven weeks on Isle Royale in winter 1996, close to the record sixty-four found in 1972. In that earlier year wolves were in on the killing and led Rolf to the carcasses; in 1996 most moose died in late winter from starvation, and their remains were usually untouched by wolves.

A huge crop of winter ticks compounded the hardship for moose in 1996. Unlike wood ticks that bother people in summer in places other than Isle Royale, winter ticks take their largest blood meal in February, and to find relief moose rub against trees and bite off hunks of their hair. This is one of three parasites that deer in the Western Hemisphere have learned to live with but that trouble and even kill moose. It's not that deer are smarter; it's just that moose are relative newcomers to our land, having crossed the Bering land bridge relatively recently. (If given enough time, some moose would figure out the advantages of grooming themselves in the fall, when the ticks climb on as tiny nymphs and take their first blood meal, rather than allowing them to build to such intolerable numbers, and those moose would survive and pass their new habit on to their offspring.) Ticks had been heavy in 1989 and 1992, and Rolf had sent a carcass to a lab in Edmonton, Alberta, where some poor technician estimated there to be more than thirty thousand ticks on one moose. Weather drives the tick cycle: ticks drop off moose in spring, and if they land on snow, they die. Warm, dry springs, such as those in 1988, 1991, and 1995, are great for ticks, and moose suffer during the following winters.

Nature dealt moose yet another blow by delaying spring. Rolf and his May Earthwatch volunteers had to hike the final mile to the island on the ice of Washington Harbor. Snow covered much of the ground until the third week of May; Trevor found a patch on the Fourth of July! In desperation, moose sought south-facing slopes, where the sun brings out the first new vegetation, but these areas produce lichens, mosses, and juniper, inedible for moose. Many moose seemed to have slipped or tripped and fallen, without the strength to get up again. One old bull broke two ribs on his last fall, and several moose seemed to have become entangled in juniper bushes.

Why weren't we seeing more evidence of wolves at these "kill" sites? Perhaps even starving moose are capable of defending themselves against wolves. More likely, there were so many of these "push-overs" that wolves didn't ever encounter most of them. Also, those starved moose had little fat for hungry wolves; perhaps a starved moose doesn't taste good. A beaver or snowshoe hare might provide a juicier meal.

In summer fieldwork in 1996, our teams recovered 226 moose carcasses. Led by our noses, we found only the most obvious ones, and few had been touched by wolves. Two bulls died within a quarter mile of each other, very near the Greenstone Ridge Trail above East Chickenbone Campground. On the park trail, between the dead moose, were two fresh wolf scats containing hair from beaver and snowshoe hare. The late spring had undoubtedly forced beaver out of their lodges and onto snow before their ponds opened up. Beaver count on spring to melt their ponds by early May. Without water for escape, beaver are sitting ducks for wolves, and beaver-on-ice is a wolf delicacy, duck soup. Beaver, even in spring, have more body fat than a starved moose, and beaver don't kick.

In the summer of 1996, I cut up a moose carcass myself, a task I had managed to avoid for twenty-five years. Rolf went to Ellesmere Island in far northern Canada for three weeks just as reports of dead moose were pouring in from park staff and visitors. One soggy, foggy morning I presented options for the day to Trevor, Joe Zanon, and Jeff Plakke, our summer crew: bake a rhubarb pie or collect either the dead moose on Ransom Ridge behind Daisy Farm, a two-mile hike, or the one near Chippewa Harbor, an eleven-mile hike. Trevor quickly chose to bake the pie, and Joe and Jeff opted for the Ransom Ridge "kill," so I suited up for the muddy hike to Chippewa Harbor.

The trip began well, though the boots that had worked well in the rain the previous week seemed to have lost their charm. As I sloshed and slipped through the mud, I met two young men from Detroit who were having a wonderful time despite a four-day rainy spell. They eagerly told me of wolf tracks on the trail ahead; these brightened the next half-mile.

The dead moose advertised itself with a now-familiar odor. It was another starved bull, lying on its side, legs outstretched where it had fallen, exhausted. A few ticks eagerly awaited a new host, so I pulled my socks over my pant cuffs and donned rubber gloves. There must be some powerful chemistry at work on a carcass, because the surrounding vegetation was rust-colored and dead, as from a burn.

Cutting off the head was easy with a sharp knife. The exposed hide was dry and tougher than jerky, but the underside was still being consumed by maggots and insects, nature's clean-up crew, and was soft. From the teeth I could tell that this bull had seen many winters. Spring had taken his last ounce of energy. I hoped it was a warm, sunny day when he died and that he didn't die shivering.

I decided not to try to get the hide off the skull. It would dull my knife, and a furry head would be less likely to break the plastic bag that lined my pack. I was already beginning to worry about the trip home. I had brought Trevor's mid-sized pack because the report was of a "little bull," but this was no midget. Later I measured his brain volume to be over five hundred cubic centimeters, one of our largest. The head could fit into the pack, the metatarsus tied on top, but if there was an arthritic pelvis, I was in trouble.

Unlike the skull, attached to the backbone by just one vertebra, the pelvis lies between the sacrum, tailbone, and two femurs, and all were covered by tough, sun-dried hide. Again, the underside was the easier half. It worked best to flip the rear half over. I found myself chatting with this old bull, apologizing for the posture I had forced him into, rear legs 180 degrees from his front ones, thanking him for donating his body to science.

After much experimentation, I put the metatarsus, with hoof and hair because the knife was now too dull for skinning, and arthritic pelvis together in a plastic bag and carried them in one arm. The five-and-a-half-mile trip on a muddy trail was dangerous now, with a heavy and unbalanced load. The air was humid and the vegetation wet; I wore raingear and got soaked from the inside.

At home I was greeted by Trevor, still at work on that rhubarb pie, and Joe and Jeff, who had found their cow moose in a similar situation as my bull, on a south-facing slope. Her skull showed osteoporotic lesions, and her upper first molars were so decayed they looked like chocolate caramels. She must have been several years overdue for her annual physical.

The moose census of 1997's winter study recorded the full extent of the devastation of the previous winter—only five hundred moose remained. Rolf counted twenty-four wolves, not the large increase one might have expected. The free lunch program for Isle Royale's wolves came too late to affect litter size because pups are conceived at the end of February or early March and are born sixty-five days later, just about when most of the moose were dying. Also, all those moose died in a very short period of time; of what use are a thousand Thanksgiving dinners, all served on one day, when you don't have a freezer? Finally, starved moose are of marginal nutritional value, especially for reproducing female wolves, who need fat. Most of those hundreds of carcasses were consumed by maggots. "What a waste!" one might say, unless one is a maggot, in which case, Grandma is still talking about the bounty of 1996.

With the young and old and sick moose culled by weather, wolves had to work hard to make a living in 1997 and 1998. Carcasses examined during those winter studies were extremely well utilized. With junk food no longer available, wolves ate good meat, and both the East Pack and Middle Pack produced litters of five pups in the spring of 1997. By winter 1998, however, all but three of those pups were dead. It seemed the supply of old, vulnerable moose was so low that the adult wolves were struggling. Rolf looked at blood samples and determined that lack of food, not disease, caused the drop in wolf numbers to just fourteen in 1998. Three collared wolves died that winter, killed and eaten by rivals from other packs.

For years after the die-off in 1996, our summer crews had great success finding bones, and our collection of bones at our summer field headquarters was quite impressive, attracting many park visitors. Some were eager to help with our project, and I was glad to put them to work. One nice man figured out why the pilot light on the refrigerator kept going out, and another helped us start a cranky old outboard motor. This latter fellow and his wife also inventoried our collection of moose incisors, the teeth Rolf uses to determine the age of a moose.

Trevor began leading Earthwatch trips in 1996. What a year to begin! Bones from a moose killed by hungry wolves are "cleaned up," but the bones of a starved moose must be extricated, a smelly, messy project. Trevor learned to share his knowledge and walk at the front of a line of Earthwatchers. Even as a youngster, he had been resourceful and level-headed during a crisis. One fiercely windy day, returning to the cabin after a dead-moose expedition, Trevor and I could see waves and wind battering our camp. The eighteen-foot skiff was lunging against its cleats on the dock, which was loose from its anchor and listing to the northeast. The wind had torn free a large section of roofing paper on the cabin, and the paper was flapping wildly. Even before we reached shore, Trevor had done "triage" and set his priorities. I simply followed his orders—"hold the ladder, hand up the nails, pull on this rope." Like his brother, Trevor loves Isle Royale; it is a source of inspiration for both boys, a place with both memories and further enticements that they can return to as long as they live.

Rolf has a hunch that the volume of a moose's brain is significant. I have my doubts but have learned to measure moose brain volume nonetheless. Using a sixty-cubic-centimeter syringe, pressure gauge, plastic tubing, and a Mickey Mouse balloon, I pump water into the balloon placed inside the cranial cavity until the pressure gauge registers three pounds per square inch. The process goes smoothly most of the time, but when a balloon bursts because of sharp protrusions inside the skull, a new setup must be made and calibrated. If the skulls sit for a few weeks in our yard, they can become housing for wasps, spiders, or garter snakes. One disgruntled beetle showed his disapproval of the brain volume project by pinching the balloon to death when it threatened to squash him.

The squeaky plastic syringe and air bubbles in the water attracted a friendly river otter during the summer of 1996. This fine fellow had been a regular visitor to our cabin in 1995 also, and Rolf reported that he had lived under Bangsund Cabin during the winter. Possibly this was one of the young otters we had watched through our window in 1991. I saw him for the first time in 1996 on a stormy evening in June, when I sat alone at the window and watched the wind whip up the harbor while lightning approached from the west. Just as the first drops of a three-inch rainfall began, the otter swam ashore and gallumphed his way under the cabin. His thumping, coughing, sneezing, and hrumphing noises in our "basement" were comforting to me that stormy night.

The next morning, he emerged at about noon, stretched luxuriously, groomed himself, and swam off. He was back in less than five minutes with a large herring in his mouth. On the dock ramp, he bit off the fish's head while the tail still flopped. Perhaps the motion bothered him, because he turned the fish around and ate the tail next, then the rest. After more grooming, he swam off, but he became a regular occupant of our downstairs quarters. He seemed to enjoy people more than his own kind and appeared at our Earthwatch banquets and Fourth of July picnic. A visitor, floating on an air mattress in Moskey Basin, yielded his perch when the otter used the air mattress as a dining table. When we replaced the cabin's linoleum and made repairs in some of the floorboards, he was on hand to inspect our work. He observed our outdoor activities, especially bone boiling. One day Trevor was sitting out front, greasing his boots, when the otter lay down, stretched out on his back and fell asleep at Trevor's feet, twitching his paws in dream.

Just a few days before we had to close up the cabin and return to town in August 1996, Rolf and I were up late one night, entering autopsy information into the computer that was hooked up to a twelve-volt battery. We heard a thump at the door, followed by the otter's hrumphing noise. We knew he had learned to open shelter doors at Daisy Farm; when Rolf opened our door he came in with the confidence of a regular guest. The shag rug just inside the door delighted him, and he lay on his back, stretching and wriggling with obvious pleasure. We continued our work while he groomed himself and explored the cabin. Finding nothing of great interest, he let himself out.

Two days later, he came inside again and repeated his luxuriating on our rug. Something outside caught his ear, and instead of going to the door, he went to the window, conveniently low, and stood on his hind legs, paws on the sill. My window box was in full bloom, and the petunias and marigolds blocked his view, so he decided to go out the door after all. This was the last time we saw the otter. Something died under our cabin during the next winter, and the smell was unusual and fishy.

Our friendship with the otter was a rare event; we have always kept our distance from Isle Royale's wildlife. The otter's death reminded me of the cost of attachment. The cycle of life and death is beautiful only if I love the whole more than any one of its parts. Yet human love, personal attachment to family and friends (including animals), is one of the best parts of being human. Love makes us vulnerable, and when the pain of separation hurts, the regularity of nature helps us handle the grief.

An otter probably doesn't ponder, let alone seek, immortality, but whether our spirits outlive our bodies has been the stuff of human poetry, philosophy, and religion for ages. Each of us is free to choose what we believe about such things, putting what we've been taught together with our own thoughts and experiences, and our perspective on death affects everything we do. Throughout my life I have tuned in to the voice of the wilderness for wisdom, and I have also discerned a still small voice within my heart. There are yet other voices. In 1997, I was awakened in the middle of the night by a phone call from my sister: "Mom died an hour ago."

Mom's death was a shock to me, even though she had suffered a major stroke three years earlier. Frustrated by her disability, she had lost her enthusiasm for life. As I sat alone with the reality of Mom's absence, I felt miraculously enveloped by her love. The words to one of her favorite poems by Eugene Field, "Little Boy Blue," came into my mind. As a child, I had thought that this was a poem about toys and stuffed animals abandoned by a child who died suddenly, and I had cried for those unhappy toys that didn't understand death. As a mother reading to my young children, my tears were for the grieving mother in the poem. Now, it seemed that Mom was telling me not to make a monument of my pain but to unlock the nursery and share the toys. "Be of good cheer and reach out to your friends; I am not far away," she seemed to say. For three years, it had seemed I was without a mother, but suddenly she was back again, bringing me encouragement and energy. Ever a good mother, she extends her love unconditionally, even now.

I had visited Mom in her nursing home a week before she died. Oblivious to the kindness of her old friends, caregivers, and other residents, she was discouraged and wanted to die. That she did not die in this frame of mind seems a miracle to me. At her memorial service, one of the nuns from the nursing home staff told me that Mom had wheeled herself to Mass just hours before she died.  Mom had been a Presbyterian, Congregationalist, and Episcopalian, but something drew her to Catholic Mass on that last day, and Sister Susan wanted me to know what the priest had said at the service, because Mom had nodded her head in agreement with his words: "People in Duluth tend to prefer certain seasons over others, but God is in all seasons, and in the same way He is with us in all parts of our lives, especially the parts we just hate." That night, Mom was sitting out in the hallway, superintending traffic while watching a nature special on TV. Nurses saw her reach out to another resident, smile, and pat her arm. It will always seem to me that Mom's heart had become an open channel once again, and love surged through her with enough power to take her earthly body and release her heavenly spirit.

In my training to be a Hospice volunteer, one of my new projects taken on after the Yellowstone sabbatical, an oncologist told me that we do not die a moment before we are, at a deep level, ready to go. I believe my mother chose her moment to depart, and about a year later my father gracefully "crossed the bar" (see Tennyson's poem by that name, a favorite of those who were born in the first decade of the twentieth century). He had spent more than a year in the dementia ward of the same nursing home where Mom had been. He had not been an easy patient. In his illness, my soft-spoken father, champion of precise language and decorum, struck out and shouted at his caregivers. One of his male nurses told me he liked dealing with my obstreperous father, that this energy was evidence of his will to live.

But during the unique occasion when my sister and brother traveled to Indonesia, Daddy stopped eating. By the time I arrived in Duluth (against his will—he had told the nurses he didn't want me to come), it was obvious what he was up to; there was an aura of calm and power about him that I had not seen in years. I told him I had come to wish him well, not to hold him back; I can only hope he heard me.

The dementia ward is a good place to die; people wander in and out of rooms, making themselves at home wherever they are. One woman sat in Daddy's reclining chair and took the chocolate I offered her. She asked me what that man in the bed was doing. When I told her I thought my dad was dying, she went to his bedside for a close look and said, "Well, that doesn't look too bad, does it?"

I sensed that my father, a dignified and private person, wanted to die alone. He seemed to have chosen this time, with my siblings as far away from Duluth as one can get, so I returned to Houghton after a three-day vigil. Somehow, it didn't seem that he was alone at all— his soul was well connected to something I couldn't sense, something beautiful and peaceful. He died the next day, and I feel his spirit with me always, loving me just as Mom does, unconditionally. He kept one of his favorite quotes, by T.S. Eliot, under the glass that covered his desk:

> They constantly try to escape
> From the darkness outside and within
> By dreaming of systems so perfect that no one will need to
> be good.
>
> — "Choruses from the Rock"

My parents were given long lives and beautiful deaths, and I did not feel as sad at their passing as I was thankful for their love and examples. Reverend Howard Anderson, the minister of Mom and Dad's church in Duluth, acknowledged my gratitude when he told me, "Sin is the failure to be joyful." Instead of focusing on the grief of loss, I concentrated on the love that was my parents, a love that is with me still.

My parents' passing prepared me for another difficult milestone: our boys leaving home for college. Just as I learned to receive love from my parents more directly, I would try to convey my love to Jeremy and Trevor in new and more effective ways. The enormity of the empty nest hit hard the first time I confronted leftover tidbits in our refrigerator. The pain reminded me of what I had felt after a miscarriage nineteen years earlier. Then, hormones brought me down quickly, and Jeremy's singing helped me rebound; now, rain and fatigue made the pain acute. Jeremy called the night Trevor left and instantly knew my heart. "Empty nest, eh, Mom?" He was sad, too, out in Yellowstone, beginning his first summer away from Isle Royale. We encouraged each other on our separate paths. Rolf's tearful low point came the next morning; he and Trevor shared several interests and personality traits. We were at the end of a wonderful era and allowed ourselves time to be sad.

Launching our sons was a major exercise in faith, and it seemed that when I had doubts, Rolf was strong, and vice versa. We chose to trust life to be good to our boys; I hoped and prayed that they would feel upheld by the love that surrounds us all, to look for the good in life. I am glad I heeded my sister-in-law's advice to stay in the nest until Jeremy and Trevor flew away. I am also glad I kept a journal so that I won't glorify the past. As Will Rogers quipped, "Things ain't what they used to be, and probably never was." As teenagers, the boys had needed less of my time but took more of my strength. The challenges were nearly overwhelming and the goal unclear, especially when we were in town, surrounded by temptations, far from nature's calming influence. It was difficult to deny our boys the things they wanted when we could afford much more than they needed. Indulgence, however, brought unstable peace. Jeremy often found my presence at home oppressive; he would have liked the use of the car, phone, and kitchen to himself. And Trevor, in the way of all youngsters, observed, "It must be nice to be a grown-up and do whatever you want all the time." Friction made it easier to let go and taught me that family doesn't always bring out the best in us.

In time, I recognized the value of the downs as well as the ups. Trevor had sensed this truth when he was about ten years old, working on an award for Cub Scouts. He had to write a prayer, which he burned into a piece of wood that still hangs on our wall, and his words expressed what he had felt while sitting on the living room couch, listening to what Jeremy and I were saying to each other in the kitchen.

> Praise the Lord for happiness
>   Thank the Lord for sadness
> and the joy that comes when the anger has passed.
>   Know that the Lord is with us.

Children watch their parents to see what life is like up ahead, and we wanted Jeremy and Trevor to know that it just gets better and better. To give our sons the best send-off, Rolf and I had to be responsible for our own happiness. If the boys constantly looked behind them to see whether the home front was okay, or if they felt we were living through their lives, they would not have been fully free to pursue their own destinies.

William Blake said it well in his poem "Eternity":

> He who binds to himself a joy
> Does the winged life destroy;
> But he who kisses the joy as it flies
> Lives in eternity's sunrise.

All the years our sons were growing up, they joined programs (scouts, church, music) that required parental involvement. This sort of work has its pitfalls, however. I often took myself and my work too seriously. One year I wrote a large enough grant proposal to give myself a small salary, and that pittance robbed me of the joy and meaning of volunteering. The obligations of the project also encumbered my time and thoughts so that I was not open to higher impulses. It can be convincingly argued that all my volunteer efforts up to this point, even though good parenting, contributed to the gap between the "haves" and "have nots." Now it was time to invest in programs that served all children.

While in Yellowstone I had cared for a friend's ten-month-old son, who reminded me of the spontaneity of small children and the significance of silliness. The love that children exude is expansive and unconditional; closeness to children is a privilege that should not be restricted to parents. To help fill our nest, at least on Saturday mornings, Rolf and I took on a "Little Brother" through the Big Brothers/Big Sisters program. We involved him in some of the wonderful community programs that had nurtured our own sons. The Legos were put into use again, and we heard another whole set of wise sayings. As we saw the beautiful soul of this boy, we did what we could to encourage the sparkle in his eye.

When Chris was ten, we invited him to spend a few days with us on Isle Royale. He settled right in, relaxing into the spirit of the place. He rowed Jeremy's boat and dug canals and harbors in our stony beach. We taught him a few card games, a new experience for him. On the last day with us, he announced he'd like to come to the island again. "Good!" I replied. "We were afraid you might get bored here." "Oh!" he said, "It is boring, but I like it anyway."

Like our "Little Brother," the elderly people I met through Hospice and volunteering at a nursing home have shared their wisdom with me. "When you are near a dying person, you'll feel you are on holy ground," I was taught. With my own father, as well as with Hospice families, I have known this phenomenon. The words that needed to be said have flown from me, without real thinking, as heart calls to heart. Why do we wait until a person is dying before treating each other with such respect? Joseph Campbell, in *The Power of Myth*, wrote that the next century must be spiritual or it won't be at all. I have experienced what Thomas Moore in *Care of the Soul* calls "daily epiphanies" when I have learned from the gifts that are placed in my path, such as the joy of sharing a poem by Edgar Guest or Longfellow with elders. When I asked one of my friends in the nursing home how she maintains her good humor, she replied, "What the hell else do I have to do? It's my new full-time job!" A forgetful mind can still be wise. She had already lost her health, husband, and home; unafraid of death, she had no worries. My elderly friend was content with her lot, free from our fast-paced culture that praises the busyness of the ant above the singing of the grasshopper, and unencumbered by the belief that humans are by nature sinful and must earn their favor with God.

During the child-rearing stage of my life, Rolf gave me a work of art consisting of an oval granite stone and a metal stick figure with arms outstretched, pushing against the stone. It was appropriate, because I was trying so hard to change the world. (I wanted "She Tried" to be inscribed on my gravestone.) But when I returned from Yellowstone, I found that the stick figure, which has cute round buttocks, can also rest on the stone and reach upward in celebration. It is a precarious position; it's much easier to topple the figure from this position than from the pushing pose, but I think this is appropriate, too, because it takes discipline to maintain a cheerful outlook.

Our children have come of age at an exciting, hopeful time. Wolves are now tolerated in areas where they were once poisoned and trapped, and they have recently been removed from the list of Endangered Species in Minnesota, Wisconsin, and Michigan. Books about simple living, bringing out the best in each other, forgiveness, and community are on bestseller lists, and people, overwhelmed by the explosion in knowledge and technology, are learning to trust "the force." Some scholars look for scientific explanations for ethical behavior, and others are finding that science, ethics, and faith are completely compatible. Children are working their way back into the center of adults' lives, and the feminine side of the human psyche is getting more press. Talk show hosts encourage us all to take responsibility for our lives and to resist the bondage of our materialistic, competitive culture. Ministers inspire us to become fully human, to receive love freely and to pass it along. As we use our technology and global perspective to act locally, we are finding powerful antidotes to despair, fear, and cynicism. Finally, people who seek justice in this world realize that loving good is more effective than hating evil.

As I let go of my parents and children, I have found more joy in loving my neighbor. No longer preoccupied with my family, I am free to notice and respond to the people that appear in my path. I once thought of Isle Royale as a refuge from people, and each spring, exhausted by the rat-race of activity and projects, I had run to the island for soul restoration. But the people I have met on the island have taught me that humans are one of God's very best things. Enveloped by the beauty and wholeness of creation, we rise to our potential and bring out the best in one another.

One summer, I allowed a painful experience from town to spoil the peacefulness I was accustomed to feeling on Isle Royale. I churned with anger and thoughts of revenge (and learned that evil voodoo doesn't work!). The island couldn't help me because my heart was not open to its messages. When I returned to town and went to church, the first sermon I heard was about forgiveness: "Do not come to the communion table until you are reconciled with your brother." The person for whom I had nursed a grudge was sitting nearby, and I asked him if we could talk later that day. Over lunch I remarked to Rolf that I was going to explain how I felt, to tell my side of the story. "Candy," Rolf replied, "I don't think you were listening to the sermon very well." Those words rattled me as I pedaled my bicycle to this fellow's home. We walked around his property for an hour or so, and as he explained what, from his perspective, had happened the previous spring, I realized that I had imagined all sorts of things that simply were not true. I had stupidly allowed my anger to fester all summer. Suddenly, after months of pain, my heart was free. It felt so good, I could have done double back-flips.

The human heart, like the chickadee brain, expands with use. Ask the parents of a large family—they may confuse their kids' names, but they never run out of love. Although our American schools have been busy developing our competitive nature, our intuitive capacity to love and to forgive has been virtually unexplored, let alone tapped. What exciting possibilities lie ahead! As I gaze at the marigolds in my window box, I am amazed by their indiscriminate generosity. Come hummingbird, sphinx moth, bumblebee, or butterfly, the response is the same—what was freely received is freely given. Courage resides in my heart, saying "Yes!" when that still, small voice nudges me to give. But my brain talks me out of all sorts of good impulses, reminding me of the cost and the danger, and so I live below my best.

For most of my life, my mind seemed to thrive on complexity; I remember my pride when, in town, I found I could cook dinner, talk on the telephone, and amuse two small children, all at once. (One night I was about to pour vegetable oil on the spaghetti when I noticed three dead mice at the bottom of the bottle!) Frenetic activity precludes reverence, however, and although successful multi-tasking sometimes brings satisfaction, this feeling is very different from the joy I derive from things I do not control or understand. Even on Isle Royale, a rigid schedule makes it impossible to enjoy a powerful storm. And fretting over my mistakes in the kitchen spoils my fun with the guests seated at the table. The storm and food are not the problem.

Isle Royale has taught me again and again that control is illusory, at best. Just as soon as we pack up for a trip, along comes a twenty-five-knot wind that prevents our use of the boat. Or, camping out for a week within earshot of wolves, we are kept awake night after night by the flapping of our tent and the rustling of leaves. Hardships and thwarted plans have forced me to revise my self-image, but when I yield control to a greater, good power, I can usually muster a positive attitude about whatever life has dished out. I am happier thinking of myself as a tiny part of a big beautiful world rather than a big shot in an imperfect world, a point on the circle rather than the apex of a pyramid (Mark Gleason's point, made in an interpretive talk on the *Ranger III*).

Humans have not always acted the way we do today. Perhaps

wolves tell the stories of their ancestors who lived with a human culture that, like theirs, was sustainable. Biologically, people are programmed to be social, and we have within us the instincts to be friendly, trusting, and generous, but we have made some bad decisions. At the age of fifteen, Jeremy observed, "We have used our powerful brains to justify actions we know in our hearts to be wrong." There are signs that we are moving towards sustainability again, and we can exercise our freedom to make choices that will benefit the common good.

A painting by Garry Meeches is the logo for the "Wolves and Humans" exhibit at the International Wolf Center in Ely. It depicts the energy of the sun flowing through a moose, into wolves and back again to the sun. Humanity's presence in the painting is only as the observer who honors the beauty and interconnectedness of creation. In Meeches' work, a powerful brain and heart are in harmony. Whether we learn to live with wolves is still uncertain, but Isle Royale offers visitors a great place to walk around in wolf country for a few days with other creatures in a relationship of mutual respect. (While we have changed our minds about wolves, it is important that they maintain their fear of us—those teeth are incredible weapons.)

Henry David Thoreau wrote, "In wildness is the preservation of the world," and I would add, "in community is the preservation of wildness." Unless we learn to live closer together, there will be no room for our fellow travelers, the wildlife. Jonathan Spence, professor of history at Yale University, has said about the civilization of China during the Ming Dynasty in the mid-sixteenth century: "They were very used to running cities with more than a million. The basic idea was that people could walk down crowded streets without getting in fights all the time; that eight people could live in a small room, covering three or four generations. . . Perhaps one of the proofs of civilization is that we can live together in large numbers in crowded spaces" (qtd. in Baker). Orlando Patterson, professor of sociology at Yale, echoes Spence's words: "An urban condition is always one in which there is greater freedom and equality. There is a German saying, 'Town air makes free.' It's no accident that all the great cultures are really urban cultures" (qtd. in Baker).

My original impression that Isle Royale is good for people (and vice versa) has been confirmed in my three decades here. I met two Duluthians on the Daisy Farm dock in 1998, waiting to board the *Voyageur II* back to Minnesota. They had shortened their trip because of the heat and felt ashamed for giving up. As an afterthought, one mentioned that they had given their stove and water filter to two fellows they had met who were ill-prepared for backpacking. "You did that?" I remarked. "You guys would make terrific next-door neighbors!" I hope they remember Isle Royale for the part of them the place brought out.

Our next-door neighbors at the Edisen Fishery for several years have been Les and Donna Mattson, wonderful people who greet the many folks who tour the fishery and lighthouse. Les and Donna appreciate the old ways of doing things, such as the use of cotton nets that are more visible than nylon ones and allow some fish to escape. Les listens politely, without even a twinge of envy, to boaters who try to impress him with their fancy gadgets. Living close to the water, he notices changes such as the lack of young herring in the stomachs of fish he catches (he blames the cormorants). Donna enjoys the hares, gulls, hummingbirds, and moose that pass through their yard. Les and Donna live fully in the present, laughing about the past and future. Pete and Laura would be pleased.

When they were eighteen years old, both Jeremy and Trevor volunteered to be the host/ranger at Daisy Farm Campground. In 1995, the Park eliminated several seasonal positions, leaving their largest campground without a shepherd, and Jeremy thought it might be fun to help smooth the feathers of boaters and hikers who sometimes have trouble sharing the place. He made bulletin boards and a reading box and put interpretive signs in outhouses, and Trevor started his evening programs by playing his violin. Teaching visitors about moose, wolves, birds, trees, and shipwrecks, our boys encouraged park visitors to focus on the island, to "look outward in the same direction." Wilderness experiences, especially in the company of strangers, remind us that, despite our outward differences, we are surprisingly similar underneath. The stratified society we have created has left our hearts unsettled. Equality is a "given" when campers are weathering a storm or blessed by a rainbow.

Life in an old fishing cabin, next-door to old-style commercial fishermen, becomes ever more enjoyable as we fall farther behind the "real world." Temptations are easily resisted. Visitors to Bangsund Cabin sometimes suggest "improvements." Certainly the place is a handyman's dream, but I love it the way it is, with inherent imperfections, like me. The cabin sits on the ground, and its lowest logs fight a perennial battle with the soil. Rolf has come to their rescue when necessary. The beauty of the cabin is its simplicity and utility. It's the only place I have ever lived where I can freely pound a nail into the wall when I need a hook. The cabin is merely a base from which we launch trips into swamps and ridges, and I hope never to lose this perspective.

Isle Royale gives us the fun of solving some problems for ourselves. Living without running water (ours walks) in the summer is really no hardship; as a matter of fact, we appreciate it more when we haul it in buckets from the lake. Modern plumbing forces us to be wasteful; the effort required to carry our clean water in and dirty water out inspires ingenious methods of water-saving. When we can pile dirty dishes in a dishwasher, we don't think about the hot water and energy that is required to clean them. Wash dishes in hot water on an 80-degree day a time or two; you will figure out how to make the process more efficient. If nothing else, you might develop some empathy for people who live with major inconvenience every day of their lives.

In 1998, our propane refrigerator acted up, and we decided to lessen our ecological footprint by getting along without it. Ice, obtained at Mott Island whenever we made a visit, and a cooler under the cedar tree worked just fine, and our propane consumption was down by half. The next summer our field assistant, Marcel Potvin, surprised us with an old restored icebox, which suits our needs perfectly. Ice cream, out of the freezer whenever you want it, is one of the blessings of town life.

For showers, we made the transition from modern plumbing gradually; perhaps living with engineers at Purdue and MTU caused us to dabble with "intermediate technology." In the early 1970s, we mounted the gas tank from an old boat six feet high on supports lashed between two trees. A rubber hose and cork controlled the water pressure. We located this set-up on the hill behind the cabin and lugged buckets of heated water fifty yards up a steep slope, over windfalls and through a dense fir stand, then climbed a rickety ladder to fill the tank. Now there was an energy-intensive invention! Today we heat a three-gallon pot of water and stand behind a tree, pouring water over ourselves with a two-cup dipper. Warmed by the sun, serenaded by warblers, I find these showers are my favorite. Why do we so often let other people's inventions rob us of elemental joy?

Although marking time on a calendar may be precise, there is satisfaction in telling seasons by the sounds and silence of birds, the flowering of orchids, the smell of witch's broom, or the thump of fir cones on the roof, cut from a branch above by a squirrel. Nature's rhythms are subtle, and it takes time to become familiar with them, but they are comforting, and the hours spent in nature's classroom are some of life's best.

My preferred method of contacting mainland friends and relatives is still paper, pen, and the U.S. mail. Speed and quantity of communication are not related to the significance of the things we say to each other, except perhaps inversely. When I make time to write, I am more thoughtful and focused, concentrating my love in one direction. At the other end, the reader approaches the mailbox with a hopeful heart, enabling magic to work through my words. A letter is never disruptive, and it can be reread, shared, and cherished. A handwritten, personal letter is a creative outlet for me, a way to care for the people I love.

Even grocery shopping is more fun when done by mail, I think. Food arrives once a week via the NPS boat *Ranger III*. I have learned that "large" means different things to different people, that baking powder comes in five-pound cans. When I ordered "meat sticks" one week, expecting to get a spicy trail snack, I received a customized package of wooden skewers. It's a rare week that I do not forget to order something, so we have learned to make do, and the resulting new recipes can be quite interesting. Inevitably, my list is a jumble of items, and I'm certain the clerk who fills my orders gets a lot of exercise wheeling a cart up and down the aisles. We have learned to be thankful for whatever we receive.

In considering the fishermen who lived on Isle Royale seventy-five years ago, I realize that their frugality and simplicity were not a matter of choice. Unlike us, these people had almost no expendable income and little free time. On moving day, I am particularly mindful of how much stuff I cart to and from the mainland each year and how

I clutter my life. Isle Royale reliably speaks with a clear voice: the freedom we seem to cherish, to do and have whatever we want, distracts us from exercising a more precious skill—to make the most of whatever we've been given. I learned this first in 1971, within the green log walls of Bangsund Cabin and through the good example of Pete and Laura Edisen, and I benefit from every annual refresher course.

Rolf and I hike as a team again, although my pace is a bit slower. The island's rocks do not seem to be changing, but moose, beaver, and plant succession are affecting familiar places. White pines are returning and will be enjoyed by visitors long after we are gone. Although we have a vast store of common memories, Rolf and I continue to maintain our varied opinions about the purpose of the Isle Royale wolf-moose research. Rolf seeks to understand the physical world; I am fascinated by our spiritual existence. Isle Royale inspires both of us to minimize our impact and maximize our praise. With luck, we will be occupied for a long time with our projects and will always remain humble before a universe that is ever marvelous.

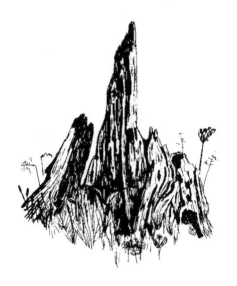

Part Four: 2000s
Embracing Vulnerability

In India, people say there are four stages in human life. For the first many years, we are students, soaking up information from our parents and teachers. The second phase is for establishing a home and raising the next generation. Next, our family circle faces outward and we make the world our home. And lastly, we "put the inner life together with the outer" (Rohr, p. 262) in preparation for the leap from this world to the next.

As I move through life's stages, Isle Royale's humble beauty does its best to help me negotiate my particular hills and valleys. Change is good, I tell myself, and then I work to see the positive side to the challenges that confront me. "The most difficult values to jettison are those that have helped you in the past," said Jared Diamond (qtd. in Joseph). It is so easy to fall into comfortable ruts and to want to stop the clock, especially when life has treated me well. And the pace of change in the world is so rapid as to be alarming. Isle Royale reminds me to take a broad view when considering the future of the world, the transitions in my family, and the relationship between my inner and outer life. The term limit imposed on each of us, as well as the events in the particular slice of history each generation experiences, help me ascribe meaning to each chapter of my life.

The world shrank abruptly for all Americans at the start of the twenty-first century. Rolf was teaching at the university and I was at home when my neighbor called: "Turn on your TV; New York City and Washington are under attack." Her daughter was a student in D.C., and Jeremy was working in Central Park. In shock, I watched the pictures of the second tower coming down, and when I heard Jeremy's cheery voice on the phone, "I'm okay, Mom!" I could barely squeak out my relief. My grief would not be personal.

For a while, it seemed some good might come of the tragedy. The world (most of it, anyway) wept with us, and Americans became like all other people, vulnerable to the violence of terrorists. It didn't take long, however, for our leaders, who saw the world simplistically, in terms of good and evil, to manipulate us, to tell us that we could regain our security through violent action, and the national mood lapsed into paranoia and vengeance ("If we don't fight them over there…"). This policy, not surprisingly, was tremendously unpopular with the rest of the world, as well as with those of us who believe a truly strong nation does not overreact to pain.

Isle Royale, remote as it is, did not escape this defensive mood; law enforcement personnel and equipment, funded with homeland security funds (borrowed, not tax-derived), became a priority. We soon had nine gun-carrying rangers on staff, and it saddened me to see Isle Royale visitors approached as potential terrorists or, at best, petty criminals. I think guns set up a barrier between staff and visitors and undermine the sense of community that Isle Royale offers. When park employees are obsessed with security, rather than service, the friendly, welcoming spirit of the island is difficult for visitors to detect. Olaus Murie wrote, "In the evolution of human spirit, something much worse than hunger can happen to a people" (qtd. in Waterman, p. 237).

Whereas September 11 jolted us onto what I consider the wrong path, climate change just might help Americans pull together, regaining our courage and sense of mission. The heating of the planet, which has affected Lake Superior and Isle Royale suddenly and dramatically, cannot be blamed on others, thank goodness. And we in the United States, who have used so much of the world's resources, can do a great good by changing our wasteful habits; by healing ourselves, the world will benefit. Regardless of the cause of the violent weather patterns we have been observing, the solutions will involve ingenuity and cooperation at every level, within and without our borders. And the changes that need to be made will also serve the cause of social justice. Again, the whole planet seems smaller, connected and vulnerable, a situation that provides humanity its greatest opportunity. Fear and vengeance have no roles to play in this drama.

The summer of 1998 ushered in a decade of summers that were hotter than average (Vucetich and Peterson). Moose are miserable when overheated, and instead of foraging and putting on the fat they need to get through the winter, they lie down in the shade. It's as though the rise in summer temperatures has come too quickly for moose to figure out how to cope. Some seek water, but a visitor saw a cow moose come to the shore of Chippewa Harbor two days in a row to stand in the cold water. The main part of her body was in the hot sun, however, and on the second day, the cow fell over, dead. Rolf performed an autopsy several days later but found nothing unusual. What does heat stroke look like?

By 2007, the effects of hot summers were obvious on Isle Royale. When I arrived in May, I saw beaches I had never seen before, and I learned the term boaters use for hitting bottom — "hard water." What had been little islands were now points, and permanent docks were so far out of the water they were useless for short people. The huge surface area of Lake Superior makes evaporation a major factor in the water level, and evaporation continues through much of the winter when, as in 2007, there is little ice. Water levels would have been even lower were it not for the massive Ogoki and Longlac dams to the north and east of Lake Superior. Built in the 1930s and 1940s, they have diverted waters destined for Hudson Bay to Lake Superior (see Annin).

At winter study that year, the warm temperatures required Rolf to fly to the island in a helicopter to determine whether there was sufficient ice (there wasn't) for Don Glaser's Super Cub to land. Once the plane arrived, windy conditions and the virtual lack of snow made it difficult to track wolves and see moose. The number of moose was the lowest ever recorded, despite a food supply that was way above average. Ticks benefit from the warming of the climate, and they were a big problem for moose during the winter of 2007; we examined an eleven-month-old calf at Windigo in May that had died of the combined effects of low fat and ticks.

(During the next winter study in 2008, conditions were superior for the moose survey, which resulted in a correction of the low estimate for the previous year. Rolf and John hired pilot Donald Murray, Jr. (yes, the grandson of Donald E. Murray), who flew the same plane his grandfather had used in the 1960s and 1970s, as a second pilot so that survey plots could be counted by two separate teams. The conditions were good, and Rolf and John have great confidence in the 2008 population estimate of 650 moose. The extremely low figure of 2007 will be called an "artifact.")

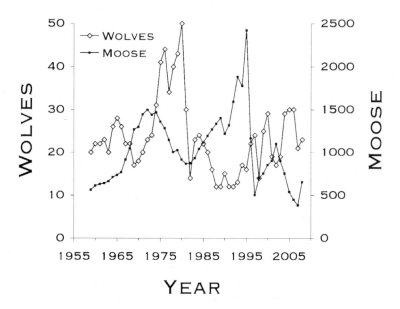

YEAR

Thus, as the project neared its fiftieth anniversary, we were in territory that Durward Allen never anticipated when he began the study in 1958. In 2007, the numbers of moose and wolves were quite similar to what had existed forty-eight years earlier, but the wolves were now in three packs, not one, and the forest was much different, with maples creeping northeastward, edible fir at the west end almost gone, and the "1936 burn," which had affected about a third of the island and produced the perfect foods for moose, grown beyond usefulness. Also, several years of drought had transformed drainages that in the 1970s had been active beaver habitat into grassy meadows, supporting a whole different cast of characters, such as sandhill cranes, rather than great blue herons. Beaver had killed the aspen and birch they needed for food and construction within a safe distance (about 150 feet) from their ponds, changing the landscape forever. Hotter summers adversely affected the moose also, changing the dynamic between them and their predators. Between 1995 and 2005, the wolf and moose populations fluctuated dramatically, emphasizing the complexity and unpredictability of natural processes. We are more humble than ever about what we understand.

We have learned that it takes time for some facts to emerge, as in the case of canine parvovirus. Not only did the disease go undetected in Isle Royale wolves until blood tests were done, seven years after it was introduced, the vector by which parvovirus was brought to Isle Royale was not known for another ten years. At a meeting of the Board of Directors of the International Wolf Center in Ely, Minnesota, Rolf spoke with a Duluth veterinarian who remembered treating the first victim of parvovirus in Duluth in July 1981. That dog had contracted the disease while celebrating the Fourth of July on Isle Royale with a dog from Chicago; it is illegal to bring dogs to the island, but two boaters had violated that rule.

Rolf is intrigued, as always, by the nature of wolf predation, which seems to change, over time, complicated by weather, insects, vegetation, and age structure. We rejoice in new knowledge that forces us to refine, and sometimes discard, our original theories. This is the excitement of science, the process of exploration, the willingness to admit that an earlier explanation doesn't tell the whole story, a belief that in time, with careful observation, we get closer to the truth.

Wolf-human relationships changed some eight to ten thousand years ago with the advent of agriculture and domestication of livestock, which involved selective breeding to create docile animals and thus eliminated the very characteristics that had protected wild prey (cattle and sheep) from wolves. With advanced technology and persistence, our ancestors were able to destroy those predators they did not like, especially wolves. People thought they were doing the right thing, but wolves suffered greatly. Those that were domesticated are still fulfilling a niche of our choosing, as "man's best friend." But in the past half century, there has been a major shift in public attitudes about the wolf, and people are now honoring its right to a place on the planet. That we can and do admit our past mistakes is a tremendous testament to the power of education. Now that wolves are re-established in several parts of our country, it remains to be seen whether we learn to live with them. We may have emerged from the mindset that had us humans evaluating all other species, encouraging the "good" ones and doing our best to eliminate the "bad," but we are susceptible to another trap in our thinking: to honor a single species rather than whole ecosystems. Those who "love" wolves need to move forward, recognizing that what wolves need is space where they are left alone and that there are some places wolves simply cannot be allowed to exist. Not until we see ourselves in a respectful relationship with all of creation will we become the best stewards. We must also remember what those jaws can do. As wolves come into contact with humans who do not threaten them, their opinion of us will likely change. We must outsmart them—never entice them with food, do not allow our children to be alone in wolf country (something I had done twenty years earlier), resist the urge to run if we encounter a wolf, and take care of our livestock and pets.

Although the story gets more complicated, we continue to enjoy sharing what we *think* we understand with all those who are interested. The sense of privilege we feel, spending so much time on Isle Royale, has only increased with time, and we welcome visitors to the cabin. I tell visitors, "If you pay taxes, you own this place as much as we do, so come on in and see what your money is doing."

Rolf made signs out of old newspapers, covered with contact paper, to greet visitors to Bangsund Cabin, especially those who stop by when we are not at home. Because the signs are "low tech," Rolf can change them as new information is learned. The gravesite, we were told by Ron Johnson, Laura Edisen's nephew, contains the remains (not much left, says the archaeologist) of between twelve and twenty miners, not just one, as we had supposed, who died in a drunken brawl between the employees of the Siskiwit and Mine Point mining companies.

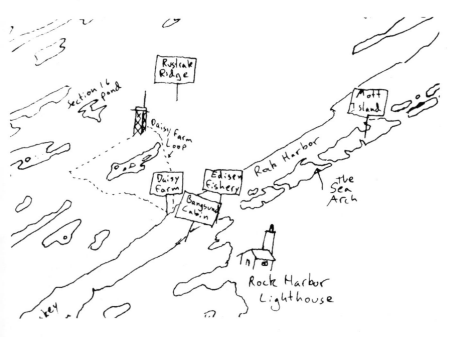

We enjoy featuring the Bangsund family, flying the Norwegian flag in their honor, and in 2002 John Bangsund, the nephew of Jack, visited and recounted more stories. He was pleased to find the cabin where he had spent his childhood intact and well loved. I jumped at the opportunity to ask John whether the Bangsund family resented our presence in their cabin and was gratified to hear his response: "Oh, no, fishing was not a way to make a living!" He remembered the economic uncertainty his parents had endured, even when times were good. He studied engineering, worked for Raytheon, and returned to Isle Royale in a fancy boat. He said he would like to write a book about commercial fishing on Isle Royale, and when I told him that Buddy Sivertsen's *Once upon an Isle* did that already, he said, "Ah, but that was about West End fishermen. Those folks were rich. Here at the northeast end, things were much different." He also said that there were four reasons for the demise of the lake trout fishery. Besides the lamprey, over-harvesting, and nylon nets, the fishermen learned, towards the end, that the female trout came to the surface just before they spawned in order to "ripen the roe." When the fishermen set their nets high in the water at that season, they caught a lot of fish. The realization that humans can affect the supply of fish in a lake as big as Superior is relatively recent.

The display of antlered skulls is the main attraction at Bangsund Cabin. Trevor built racks for the 140-plus fellows in the back yard to get them off the ground. (Rolf puts the skulls away in a storage shed each winter to preserve them.) We know quite a bit about some of these bulls, and we enjoy sharing their stories. Although Isle Royale moose have relatively small antlers (islands tend to create large numbers of animals, not large animals), the spectacle of so many together is impressive, as is Rolf's interpretive guide to the bulls with unusual antlers. Because Isle Royale bulls are not hunted, their antlers are able to grow old and asymmetrical.

We have kept a guest book since 1997 to help us remember the people who have visited. We often talk about more than wolves and moose. History, religion, and politics are important to me, and I enjoy relating these topics to the work Rolf is doing. Science must be communicated to the public for at least two reasons. First, the study is supported by public funds, and scientists are accountable to those whose taxes support it. Second, because democracy presupposes an educated electorate, science must inform the public so that good decisions are made. From what people have written in our guest book, it seems that Isle Royale speaks to its visitors in various ways, and, in general, people leave the park feeling better informed, refreshed, and hopeful.

It seems to me that many people have lost faith in themselves and each other. If I have learned nothing else from Isle Royale, it is that nature is essentially good, and it stands to reason that if butterflies, fir trees, moose, and wolves are good, certainly people are, too. (I continue to believe our compassionate hearts are our best part. Were humans an endangered species, would wolves lift a paw to save us?) For some reason, however, we hide our gentle and generous nature behind various facades; our masks become a bad habit and our unexercised good parts are allowed to wither. Wide disparities in wealth and power seem to exacerbate this problem, but part of an Isle Royale experience is equality in our relationships with other people. Encompassed and inspired by the beauty of nature, people feel free to shed their phony exterior. I see hopeful signs in the big world, too: strong women, now accepted, are making the world a better place for gentle men. Perhaps what makes for sainthood is the courage to expose oneself, to be vulnerable, trusting that the goodness in oneself will meet with the goodness in others.

As NPS priorities changed, favoring law enforcement rather than interpretation, I volunteered to give evening programs at Daisy Farm. My long history with YWCA and YMCA camps taught me the importance of "evening devotions," a gathering of folks for a conversation about something important. I begin by honoring those visitors who hike on trails and stay in campgrounds, giving more space to the wolves and moose. Often moonrises or rainbows over Middle Island Passage, moose ambling through the campground, or singing loons change the focus of the evening. I prefer discussions to lecture and always manage to work in a theme of reverence toward nature, including humans. What we believe affects everything we do and say, and it is worth articulating our thoughts, bouncing them around in respectful dialogue. For example, if one thinks of this world as a battleground where the forces of good and evil are constantly fighting, one can justify exclusiveness, even violence. In contrast, I believe there are really only two forces at work in this world, love and fear, and that love is, slowly but surely, overcoming fear.

A Course in Miracles is a program that looks at Christianity in a new way, and part of its wisdom is this: "At all times, and in all situations, we are either extending love or calling for love." This is even more than turning the other cheek—it involves active, positive engagement with the person who has just hurt me. I heard of a woman who was out jogging and, her mind on other things, suddenly found herself in a "bad" neighborhood. Sure enough, she heard the sound of heavy footsteps approaching her from behind. She was a small woman and knew there was no way to avoid physically interacting with this person. Taking a deep breath, she turned and faced, yes, a big man, and said to him: "I am really scared. Would you mind walking with me until I get back into familiar territory?" The man agreed, and she later learned that her trust in him had transformed his life. He had had bad intentions, but her ability to see the goodness in him had changed his life.

For me, knowing God involves more than the peak experiences, the awesome sense of oneness with all creation. When riding the crest of a wave, heady with pride and confidence, it is easy to love myself and the world. I fill my life with activity and my own voice. But it is when I am at my lowest points that I am open to the healing powers within and around me. At these times, I have not lost my faith in life's goodness, but I have felt unworthy, cut off from the beauty. It has been important to suffer through these awful times; there is no way to shortcut grief. And before I can know the joy of wholeness and blessing, I must acknowledge my mistakes and become soft and vulnerable. Eventually, love, beauty, and goodness flood into my heart, and it occurs to me that the processes of healing are far more powerful than my mistakes and shortcomings. With renewed courage, I get up, dust myself off, and get on with the life-long project of joyous praise and thanksgiving.

There is a traditional Hawaiian healing process called ho'oponopono that arises from an interconnected worldview and helps people cleanse themselves of the judgments, beliefs, and attitudes that create divisions in our families and communities. The purpose is to regain our inborn divinity and wholeness, something we lose sight of because of our errors in thought, word, and action. Ho'oponopono seeks to release us from the burdens of hurtful memories that we run and rerun in our minds. A challenging aspect of ho'oponopono is this:

since I am connected to the whole world, my behavior affects the health of the whole world, and I am thus responsible for the problems I see. This is heavy, but it also holds out huge possibilities because when I heal myself, I heal the world. How to know what faults to work on? I notice the voice of judgment and remember that when I point my finger at someone else, three fingers are pointing at me. Then, I identify the source of the problem in myself (this takes effort!) and say to myself, "I'm sorry. I love you."

Hearkening back to Thomas Moore, I believe our era is becoming more spiritual, and ideas like the one just mentioned encourage my faith that we humans are becoming more responsible for our behavior. Instead of acting like sheep, easily frightened by the media and following leaders without asking where we are going, we are realizing a few things—we can all go forward together in a sustainable relationship with nature, and powerless people have few options other than violence.

A recent visitor, a retired Methodist minister, spoke with me after one of my programs and related a piece of wisdom he had learned on the worst day of his life, when he was told he needed open heart surgery and his wife had incurable Parkinson's disease. "Please, God, if you have anything to tell me, now would be a good time," he remembers praying that evening. The words that came to his heart were these: "You will do your best, and trust that you have always done so." We can do a lot by embracing and passing along this blessed assurance.

Sitting on a beach in a national park, we talk about the experience of sharing public land, where nobody needs a key or credit card and nobody frets about the chores of home ownership. We are all winners here, a rare feeling in our competitive society. Sharing a pubic park is a little like attending an inspiring lecture or concert, after which we all go home with something in common. Our joy is not diminished in the parking lot, where we meet someone who was rooting for the losing team. And sharing a bond with strangers awakens a part of our hearts that can always use more exercise.

I remember that my courses in economics taught me to think in terms of scarcity: given a fixed supply, the price increases with demand. But from Isle Royale, looking at the boundless sky, we open our hearts to a larger scale, thinking in Carl Sagan's terms: billions of stars, millions of galaxies. The whole is more than the sum of its parts, a much more empowering and hopeful perspective than what I remember from classical economic theory.

From Isle Royale's perspective, our materialistic lifestyle back home seems a trap. Our yearning to feel connected to nature and to each other conflicts with a lifestyle that promotes isolation from and competition with our neighbors. Surely our forefathers didn't expend all their energy and wisdom for our freedom to consume without limits, to pamper ourselves at the expense of the common good, and to pursue security and safety as our national and personal passion. We are capable of so much more! Daniel Quinn put it well: "The people of our culture don't represent the final stage of human development" (p. 110). As a Christian, I think of what a positive difference my religion could have made in the world in the past two thousand years had its emphasis been on peace with justice (which necessarily involves wise environmental policies) rather than personal salvation. But here again I see a possibility opening up—instead of working for a good seat in the next world, many religious people are putting their energy into making this world more like heaven.

We could certainly use leaders to inspire us to do what we know in our hearts is right, such as use mass transit, build smaller homes with more efficient plumbing and heating, overcome our fears about people who are different from us, participate in public decision-making, and so on. Until that leader emerges, we must all pitch in, however we can, counting on our desire to do the right thing, a characteristic we all have in common. Education is leading us forward, and as we realize the mistakes we have made, we change. When I was a child, on canoe trips in northern Minnesota, my mother, a Girl Scout leader who cared deeply for wild land, burned our cans and then sank them in the lake, following the advice of Forest Service rangers. I hate to think how much metal we dumped in those lakes! But we thought we were doing the right thing! At Daisy Farm, I advise people not to slam shelter or outhouse doors and to notice how it feels to do something that helps others, anonymously. Part of the Isle Royale experience is the good feeling of acting within the impulses and confines of conscience.

"A man should never be ashamed to own he has been in the wrong, which is but saying, in other words, that he is wiser today than he was yesterday," said Alexander Pope. I have changed what I tell visitors about natural selection when I give tours of our bone yard. Whereas arthritic vertebrae, jaw infections, and broken bones attest to the selectivity of wolf predation in a natural ecosystem, we humans have done what we can to remove ourselves from that evolutionary process. People pass along genetic problems, generation after generation. Years ago, I felt this was a major problem, but one day, while giving the tour to a person with severe physical disabilities, I realized the narrowness of that view. Our best part is not our physical potential but our spiritual capacity.

One morning in July, I was cleaning metatarsal bones in the front yard when I looked up to see a huge three-masted sailing ship setting its anchor between our cabin and Daisy Farm. The captain zipped to our dock in her Zodiac to make us a bargain: if she and her crew could see our moose bones, we could tour their ship. What a deal! The *Denis Sullivan* is the flagship of the State of Wisconsin, and it carries groups of people (who participate as members of the crew) for various expeditions on the Great Lakes. The next evening they invited us to see a movie: "Around Cape Horn." It was filmed in 1929 but narrated in 1980 by Captain Irving Johnson, who kept repeating the phrase, "the cargo must get through." Two sailors were swept overboard in a storm, but barely any mention was made of them. The ship was carrying nitrates from Chile as part of the secret re-arming of Germany, yet all the crew felt the mission to be sacred. Actually, most of the crew probably didn't even know what was in the hold.

Fifty years later, it seemed the captain continued to believe in the mission. I guess it has always been easy to lose one's perspective. I remember Olaus Murie's last words, "You know, we have to find out what we're here for. That's what life is all about" (qtd. in Waterman, p. 177). The captain and crew were products of their time, in denial of the fact that when one group wins at the expense of another, bitter resentments are created, and the cycle of violence continues.

In the fourth decade of research, in addition to the long-term monitoring of the wolf and moose populations, several other studies have been done by graduate and undergraduate students. Leah Vucetich showed that mice that were confined to small islands in Rock Harbor had less genetic variability and poorer survival than those living on the big island. Leah has since learned to extract and analyze DNA from wolf scats, hair, and other tissue, and this technique allows us to monitor the life span of individual wolves on Isle Royale without having to handle the animals. She is also studying the hair-loss patterns due to winter ticks on moose. Keren Tischler demonstrated that the aquatic plants moose eat in summer are extremely high in protein. She used stable isotopes of carbon and nitrogen to estimate that aquatic plants make up as much as a third of the summer diet of moose. Madeline Campbell showed how young balsam fir trees have diverged on the two ends of the island: at the east end, growth is normal, but at the west end, trees are stunted and do not produce cones because they are so heavily browsed. Ken Mills measured the antlers of all those specimens in the back yard (he spent much of one summer devising a way to measure antler volume; standard measurements don't work) and found that Isle Royale moose have the smallest antlers of any moose population in the world. He also measured the volume of the antlers of old bulls and found that they become smaller and less symmetrical after prime age (about ten). Jason Deutsch devised a method of determining the sex of a moose skeleton by measuring an angle in the pelvis. Joseph Bump is studying the significance of nutrient recycling from carcasses, making comparisons between Isle Royale and Yellowstone, and between wolf-killed and starved prey. A new project is to become more sophisticated in our assessment of date of death when we find carcasses in our summer hiking. Marcel Potvin studied wolf activity patterns and found that attendance at den sites was unpredictable and unrelated to the density of moose. John Vucetich has published several papers and is interested in everything. One paper, on the relationship between wolves and ravens, suggests that the presence of ravens, on the planet long before wolves or moose, probably led to wolves living in packs, so that more of their food goes to other wolves, not to scavengers (Vucetich, Peterson, and Waite).

Unlike the wolf packs Marcel studied, our family showed a regular and predictable activity pattern around our den site, Bangsund Cabin.

As their wings gained strength, Jeremy and Trevor found other home bases and new friends. Isle Royale has been a source of strength for each of us in different ways. The reunions on the island, though infrequent, are wonderful.

Jeremy called us in town late one night in 1998 from somewhere along the Pennsylvania turnpike. He had been driving for two days in his little red MGB, trying to get from his summer job in Yellowstone National Park to an important first class of his senior year at Swarthmore College. Tired, wet, and frightened, he called for advice about his route, wondering if the smaller roads would have fewer big trucks. We got out an atlas and a magnifying glass and squeezed our sleepy eyeballs to focus on a map of Pennsylvania. I asked him if he were alone. "No, I'm at a truck stop," he replied. "Good," I said. "Now talk to the waitresses and truck drivers and get their advice." I then lay awake the rest of the night, wondering how he was doing, sending my love. In the morning he called to say he'd made it. In time, he will accumulate enough of these experiences to trust life's goodness, and until that day comes, I will uphold him with my faith.

To a Waterfowl

> Whither, 'midst falling dew,
> When glow the heavens with the last steps of day,
> Far, through their rosy depths, dost thou pursue
> Thy solitary way?
>
> Vainly the fowler's eye
> Might mark thy distant flight to do thee wrong,
> As, darkly painted on the crimson sky,
> Thy figure floats along.
>
> Seek'st though the plashy brink
> Of weedy lake, or marge of river wide,
> Or where the rocking billows rise and sink
> On the chafed ocean side?
>
> There is a Power whose care
> Teaches thy way along that pathless coast —
> The desert and illimitable air, —
> Lone wandering, but not lost.
>
> All day thy wings have fanned,
> At that far height, the cold, thin atmosphere,
> Yet stoop not, weary, to the welcome land,
> Though the dark night is near.

And soon that toil shall end;
Soon shalt thou find a summer home, and rest,
And scream among thy fellows; reeds shall bend,
Soon, o'er thy sheltered nest.

Thou'rt gone, the abyss of heaven
Hath swallowed up they form; yet, on my heart
Deeply hath sunk the lesson thou hast given,
And shall not soon depart.

He who, from zone to zone,
Guides through the boundless sky thy certain flight,
In the long way that I must tread alone,
Will lead my steps aright.

— William Cullen Bryant

Jeremy returned to the island in 2000 to lead an August Earthwatch team, and in 2002 he visited just before moving to Argentina for a year. He had decided to go to law school but wanted to look at the world from outside the borders of his native country. He happened to be on the island at the same time as a group of journalists, and one of the leaders encouraged him to volunteer for the English-speaking newspaper in Buenos Aires. Jeremy took that tip, and his work for the *Buenos Aires Herald* inspired him to write a book about Robert Cox, who had been the paper's courageous editor during the "Dirty War" in Argentina in the late 1970s.

The following June, Jeremy came to Isle Royale from Argentina, bringing a beautiful young woman, Maria. On her first evening on the island, we all hiked to Ojibway Tower, and while on the roof listening to wolf radio-collar beeps, we saw the alpha pair of the East Pack come up the trail from the southwest. It seemed a huge blessing, a positive sign, and we were delighted when Jeremy and Maria told us, two months later, of their engagement. Immigration has not been easy since 9/11, and there were lots of delays because Jeremy and Maria wanted to do everything properly. In November 2004, they were married in Formosa, Argentina, which sits on a huge freshwater aquifer on the border with Paraguay. Instead of taking a honeymoon, the newlyweds spent several days serving as interpreters so that their parents could become acquainted.

Trevor's separation from Isle Royale was gradual, also. After a summer as the volunteer at Daisy Farm, he held a Resource Management position for the park. Living at Mott Island headquarters was not easy for him, but he took advantage of the electricity and acoustics of the carpenter shop to record himself playing the fiddle, mandolin, and keyboard. He led an Earthwatch trip in August. The next summer he worked at Acadia National Park in Maine, again for Resource Management, and tried, as the new kid on the block, to convince long-term visitors of the presence of rabies in park raccoons. In 2001, he did a research project on Kent Island, on the border between Maine and New Brunswick, Canada, but he was able to come to Isle Royale for another canoe/kayak adventure with us. In 2002, he and his lovely girlfriend Sarah were the campground hosts on Jewell Island in Casco Bay, Maine. The following summer, Trevor brought Sarah to Isle Royale in September. She, like Maria, brought us good luck—we heard wolves howl as we hiked from Lake Richie to Moskey Basin. Sarah joined the family in August 2005, and the newlyweds continue to live in Maine, where Trevor works for an environmental consulting firm and Sarah is an environmental educator.

Seeing our sons happily married is a source of great joy for us and seems an affirmation of what we tried to teach them—to trust, to follow their bliss, to courageously commit themselves to other people through marriage. We did as much as we could for our sons, but Maria and Sarah are bringing out the best in them, and vice versa. We trust that all four of these young people will continue to experience the freedom and empowerment that we have found in marriage.

I rejoice that our children are better suited to the current world than I am, and I treasure the lessons they continue to teach me. One fall, when Rolf and I returned to Houghton, we discovered some vandalism (destroyed benches) at the school forest where we have put in a lot of volunteer effort. Rolf was inclined to let the place go benchless for a year, but we talked with Jeremy, working at the time for the New York City Parks Department, who said, "You must fix things up right away. You've got to forgive the vandals and make repairs so that people don't get used to seeing broken things."

Jeremy's initial assignment at the Parks Department had involved handling angry phone calls from disgruntled park users. He liked the work: "Angry people are so interesting," he said. I recalled the many afternoons he had come home from school to "push my buttons," and I finally understood the silver lining in that cloud.

In August 2003, between the visits of Maria and Sarah to Isle Royale, Rolf's mom, who had been failing gradually from heart/lung problems (she grew up in the plume of a coal processing plant in St. Paul), passed from this world. At her memorial service, we sang "This Is My Father's World," and I felt that her soul was free and at peace in the natural world of northern Minnesota, a place she dearly loved.

The following week, Rolf and I were paddling on the south shore of Isle Royale, trying to circumnavigate the island in nine days. Strong winds and high waves forced us to change our plans (on day six we were not even to Long Point), and as soon as we decided to turn back the trip improved. The waves no longer seemed sinister and threatening, only playful and beautiful, and I felt Rolf's mom's spirit was guiding us. She *never* complained about roadblocks or challenging weather, and she understood that striving for perfection is full of ego and activity and has nothing to do with reverence and praise. She was perfect in her love, and her example is a beacon for me.

For four years, beginning in 2002, a group of journalists visited Isle Royale as part of an Institute for Journalism and Natural Resources, the brainchild of Frank Allen, formerly a reporter for *The Wall Street Journal*. Environmental problems tend to be underreported in the media because they require a great deal of time both to understand and to communicate to the public. In the Great Waters Institute, fourteen journalists from around the country were given a ten-day tour and were informed about issues such as diversion of Great Lakes water, the effects of mining, paper mills, and power plants on the watershed, and the usefulness of abandoned copper mines as habitat for hibernating bats. After an intense week, the group came to Isle Royale, where they could let their new knowledge sink in while being reassured that the healing processes of nature are alive and well.

In 2003, Rolf took a sabbatical so that we could be on the island from late April through October. On May 24, while camped in a shelter at Windigo, we were awakened by a very strange sound, like the breathing of Darth Vader. Rolf figured out that we were listening to a cow in labor at the edge of the creek just below the shelter. At four o'clock in the morning, we couldn't see a thing, but we could hear the bleating of a newborn calf. We spent much of the next day with the new family, watching the mother cross the creek to feed, leaving the little one alone for hours at a time. (Did she consider us competent babysitters?) When she visited the calf, she tried to get it to cross Washington Creek, but the calf, perched on a rather high bank, was not ready for diving lessons. Eventually the cow led her tiny newborn to a better launching site, and the calf cooperated. After its first swim, it seemed quite proud of itself and almost pranced along the far shoreline and then into the woods.

On the last day of September of that same year, a cow moose died in Daisy Farm Campground. We had heard this "gravelly voiced cow" for a few days, and campers had reported that she, although really thin, was being courted by a bull. Wolves were nearby, and she lay down as close as she could get to a campground shelter, where she expired that night. Rolf didn't want wolves coming into the campground, and he found a dozen willing volunteers to help him haul the carcass into the woods, where he performed an autopsy. The cow had a massive infection in her lungs and heart, and later we found that she had some sort of malady that affected all four distal leg bones — they were covered with excess bone in a lacey pattern. Doctors who have seen the bones surmise that the cow had a parathyroid gland malfunction. She was twelve years old and suffered from arthritis. Judging from her voice in those last days, she was ready to die, but I hope she had a bit of fun on her last night.

In October, we spent five days on the Feldtmann Loop, a trip we had not done for about thirty years. On our first night, in the campground at Feldtmann Lake, we watched the full moon rise and listened to the Middle Pack of wolves howl nearby. The following morning, we met a fellow in the next tent site who was the chaplain in a juvenile prison in the Chicago area. He, too, had felt blessed by the moonlight and wolf song as he began his first adventure on the island. The next night, we camped in a really lousy spot at the east end of the lake; Rolf said a former graduate student had camped there often, but he had not needed much space. That night also was memorable because of the loud squawking of a young great horned owl, a sound we had heard on rare occasions but had not been able to identify. On the third day, we revisited some of our favorite places on Feldtmann Ridge, where we met the Chicago chaplain again. He had learned the Isle Royale pace (slow) and was having "the best vacation of my life." That night we camped at Siskiwit Bay, and I remember waking up in the middle of the night and noticing an interesting pattern as the moonlight came through the mosquito netting: the moon was at the center of a cross of light, just like Jesus' cross, and it seemed the perfect combination of natural and Christian symbols. The next day, we poked around the ruins of Island Mine, a good demonstration of phenomenal human ingenuity that could not overcome logistical obstacles. On our last day, while hiking into Windigo, we watched a large bull moose with polished antlers run from us, and I may never understand why a prime bull fears people.

Staying on the island through the fall was so delightful that the next August, while packing up to move back to town, Rolf decided to give notice to MTU of his intention to retire in June 2006. He would be only fifty-seven years old, but the time to transfer the direction of the project to his colleagues, John and Leah Vucetich, seemed right for everyone. Rolf would continue to be involved in every aspect of the research project but would step down from commitments at the university. A change in leadership at MTU (the new president had been the dean of the School of Forestry) gave Rolf the confidence that his position would not succumb to budget cutting. John felt his resume was strong enough for him to compete with other candidates for Rolf's position, and Rolf was ready to taste the freedom he had given me for thirty years. I think I was as excited as Rolf about his retirement. At the beginning of the baby boom retirement crowd, we represent a generation that had careers we chose, jobs that did not wear us out. We have a lot of energy and idealism, and we are ready to support the next generation, better able than we are to think outside the box. There is much more to Rolf O. Peterson than was expressed through his job at the university. He's an artist whose talents are just beginning to emerge through painting. Most people won't see any change in Rolf as a retiree, however, because he will continue to be involved in the Isle Royale research, winter, spring, summer, and fall.

In 2006, more visitors to Isle Royale saw wolves than ever before. With numbers of moose very low, wolves were hungry, and they seemed to come to campgrounds to look for moose, especially cows with calves that seek protection by staying close to humans. Rolf hoped that the "fearless" wolves were an anomaly—hungry, daring yearlings, perhaps. By winter 2007, there were ten fewer wolves in the population, and it seemed that the "problem" wolves were gone, for the time being anyway. It is vital that wolves and humans keep their distance from one another.

We continue to use Earthwatch volunteers to help us find moose bones, and they have made such important contributions that in 2007 we decided not to hire summer field assistants. Park staff and visitors, using GPS technology, now bring us accurate reports of skeletons, and Rolf and I, now on the island for so much of the year, are able to visit the reported sites and collect the bones ourselves. While I miss having young people as part of our summer family, I understand budget constraints, and I appreciate my new freedom.

No matter how long we are on the island, I am never eager to leave the place where I am able to be fully present, whether hiking, sitting at the cabin window, entertaining visitors, or measuring moose bones. In addition, I'm always aware of geological time, the day and night sky overhead, the processes of forest succession and evolution all around me. Sometimes I feel even more connected to my family and friends while physically separated from them, and I can send loving energy to them when they are struggling with crises. As my yoga teacher says, "A lighthouse does not run all over an island looking for boats to save; it just stands there shining." Grateful for all my blessings, I continue to see myself as "support crew" for other people's good projects.

Just as Isle Royale helped me learn, raise our children, and become a citizen of the world, it now seems to be guiding me as I confront my own mortality. Old things die and are replaced by new life, improved by the process of natural selection. To see the good in the changes is the challenge, always. The beauty of life's cycle derives from the finite limits of time and space allotted to every living thing. Think of the energy we put into denying and forestalling the aging process! Imagine, if we lived forever, all the Hallmark cards we would have to remember to send. Birth would not be special, rebirth unheard-of, and life would be unimaginably tiresome. I remember the words that spoke to my mother's heart on her last day: all stages of life have merit.

In March 2006, Jeremy and Maria presented us with our first grandchild. As I looked into those perky new eyes, uplifted, expectant, confident in the love that produced him, I marveled at the original blessing endowing each new life. A friend gave me an interesting little book years ago by Fynn called *Mister God, This Is Anna* in which the protagonist, a five-year-old girl, says, "It is not the evil in humanity that makes man a lonely creature. It is the goodness in him that cannot get out, that does not reach to the goodness in others." A newborn baby, so vulnerable yet fearless, has the power to bring out the best in every human being. Marianne Williamson's words could be read at the birth of every child:

> Our deepest fear
> Is not that we are inadequate.
> Our deepest fear is that we are powerful beyond measure.
> It is our Light, not our Darkness, that most frightens us.
> We ask ourselves: who am I to be brilliant, gorgeous, talented, fabulous?
> Actually, who are you not to be?
> You are a child of God.
> Your playing small does not serve the world.
> There is nothing enlightened about shrinking so that other people won't feel insecure around you.
> We are born to make manifest the glory of God that is within us.
> It is not just in some of us, it is in everyone.
> And as we let our own Light shine, we unconsciously give other people permission to do the same.
> As we are liberated from our own fear, our presence automatically liberates others.

I have a minister friend, a regular Isle Royale visitor, who always asks me why wolves must kill moose in order to live. I have suggested to him that, were I a moose, I would rather die quickly from wolves than slowly and painfully with hurting teeth or joints, and it would be comforting to know that my body would be recycled into something "new and improved." Nature's winnowing always moves towards healing and wholeness. "But why must creatures suffer?" continues my minister friend. I told him about endorphins and explained that moose that have been wounded and are surrounded by wolves seem to go into a state of shock before they are actually killed by wolves. For humans, perhaps the point of suffering is to force us into each other's arms. Our tendency to compare ourselves to others, and our knowledge of the possibilities available can add to our misery when times are tough. In his "Letter to the Romans," Paul wrote: "suffering produces endurance, and endurance produces character, and character produces hope." It seems we suffer when we feel abandoned and alone, an experience all humans share at different times. It happened to Jesus on the cross, and in that brief moment when he cried out, "My God, why hast Thou forsaken me?" he suffered. I have always liked the last verse of Leonard Cohen's song "Suzanne":

> And Jesus was a sailor, and he walked upon the water,
> And He spent a long time watching from a lonely wooden tower,
> And when He knew for certain only drowning men could see Him,
> He said, "All men shall be sailors then, until the sea shall free them."
> He himself was broken, long before the sky would open,
> Forsaken, almost human, He sank beneath your wisdom like a stone.

In a spiritual sense, this life is only part of our experience. We are given opportunities to make our lives meaningful, to overcome challenges, to learn to live with insecurity, to find out who we are and how we are related to everything else, and to heal others by healing ourselves. When we glimpse the big picture, we experience the "peace that passes all understanding," and we can have more of these experiences as we age as long as we keep open minds and hearts, resisting the ideas that create and exacerbate our fears.

Now that Rolf is retired, I spend half of each year on Isle Royale. Even so, it is difficult to maintain a healthy perspective when I return to the "real" world. Recently, a new thought is helping me put my two very different lives together. I have spent Sundays my whole life (when not on Isle Royale) in churches (Congregational, Episcopal, Lutheran, Methodist) that proclaim "God Is Love" on banners in either the sanctuary or fellowship hall. When I was a child, Bible stories, stained glass windows, and beautiful music helped me understand a love that was different from what I received from my family and friends. Through education and experience, my faith has continuously evolved, becoming ever more inclusive and powerful. God is love, indeed.

I was never taught fear, which opposes love, in church. I learned that in other places, like movie theaters, the evening news, magazines, school, and doctor and dentist offices. At church, I only heard that love casts out fear, and that every problem could be made manageable if I let love, not fear, rule my heart.

Coming of age in the 1960s, I was exposed to great ideas from other cultures. The more exotic the author's picture on the book jacket (Gibran, Gandhi, Zora Neale Hurston), the more electric was the discovery that we all yearn for the same things. The teachings of Jesus (love God and neighbor) have held up well in comparison with other religions, and it still seems to me that Jesus, more than any other person in history, realized the divinity that is possible in all of us.

It has occurred to me that God, who is love, is also the physical force of attraction that works to pull all matter together. But what counteracts gravitational force, working in the way fear does to oppose love? Recently, a physicist told me that there is no fundamental force in nature that opposes gravity. Wow! We live within God's love and gravity, forces that will prevail, no matter how long we try to resist them. All the walls we erect, including belief systems, will crumble.

I believe human history is a gradual progression. Despite a few major setbacks, humanity as a whole has moved steadily from tribalism toward diverse and vibrant community. Technology has enabled the transportation and communication essential for intercultural understanding. Our nation is blessed with phenomenal diversity and a remarkable legal system that is itself evolving in the direction of inclusiveness and empowerment. We believe that universal public education is required for self-governance and that scientific knowledge enhances our reverence for life. If our community is to be sustainable, however, we must not confuse our wants and needs. Lanza del Vasto, an Italian follower of Gandhi, exhorts: "Strive to be what only you can be; strive to want what everyone can have." And we must use the gadgets of communication responsibly, 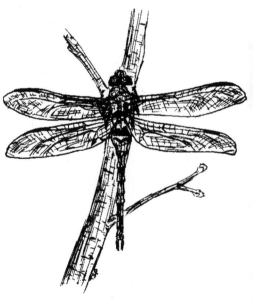 recognizing and resisting the messages that are intended to make us hate others. (In the Baha'i faith, gossip is the worst sin.)

97

Rolf speaks of Isle Royale as an outdoor laboratory, but that image does not work for me because a laboratory excludes the general public, for whom the parks were established. Also, labs are for tinkering, and the island is a natural park, a look-see sort of place; tinkering is not allowed. I much prefer to think of Isle Royale as a circus, the best sort of circus, because nature runs the whole show. People come to the circus for many different reasons; the wolf-moose drama occupies only one of several rings. There are clowns, and otters are primary in this role. We humans are in the audience, vital to the whole performance. Rolf is in the audience, too, watching and describing what is going on with the wolves and moose, sharing his findings with anyone who is interested. The park maintenance staff makes sure our seats work, and rangers serve as ushers—the interpretive rangers help visitors understand and appreciate the island, and the enforcement officers make sure we don't interfere with the show or prevent each other from enjoying the performance. Not everyone is watching the same thing—some come to dive on shipwrecks, some come to fish or hike or photograph wildflowers—but as long as you respect my interest, and I yours, we get along just fine. Sometimes a spectacular display of northern lights or howling wolves has us all rise from our seats, and then we realize how very good it feels to share an awesome moment. The differences that may have divided us earlier in the day—your noisiness or my smelly t-shirt—fade as we receive blessings together. We aren't bothered by the closeness of the seats because we have become less irritable and less irritating. And when we are afraid, it is nice to have someone sitting in the next seat. This realization, this deep connection to other human beings as well as to the wilderness, is the most special gift Isle Royale can offer.

The fact that nobody owns the island circus is significant. The enjoyment we experience is enhanced because we are not distracted by concerns and temptations that inevitably accompany private ownership. And it feels so good to share our "oohs and aahs" and laughter with strangers. Finally, both the animals that perform for us and the land we share are protected by law. Public lands offer people an opportunity to practice collective stewardship; acting together, we have different priorities than when determining the future of our own private property.

We are a funny creature. We think we want to be in the ring, receiving accolades from the audience. But the ring is a lonely place, and our ego trips have short-lived benefits and long-term costs. The joy of looking outward together, laughing or marveling at what we see, actually feels better than being in the limelight. Sometimes, in the stands, we are so overwhelmed by the beauty we have seen that we must express our joy — through art, music, or hugging our neighbor. We might even rush out for a moment into the ring. The trick is to know when to return to our seats!

Many of us stop going to the circus when we become adults. We say that we have more important things to do, such as earning money for tickets, forgetting that these performances are free. Sometimes we stay away from the circus because we are grieving over the loss of a loved one, but at this circus those who have passed on have front row seats, and we can feel close to them when we attend the next performance. Some of us become preoccupied with selecting "the best" seats, and others of us are so busy fiddling with camera equipment that we miss the action, forgetting that the circus is continuous and live performances are far better than videotapes. Sometimes we are distracted by the toys we bring with us (have you noticed how we love to compare our camping gear?) or the games we play with each other in the stands. Fortunately, in a public park, when my activity disrupts your enjoyment of the show, the staff will keep me in line.

And Isle Royale is not the only show in town. Many people, perhaps most, would never want to come to this place I love so much. This is good, because the island cannot handle many visitors. But I am certain everyone is capable of feeling the way I feel when here, and I encourage people to continue to search for experiences that keep their inborn sense of wonder alive, reassuring them that we all are significant players in life's adventure. Art galleries, museums, concerts, as well as other public lands might all be considered circuses.

The temperature under Isle Royale's big top is rising. All the performers are affected, but the humans in the audience are the only ones that might be able to do something to change this trend. In the process, we can ennoble ourselves, embracing the unknowns of the future with hope, changing the myriad things we can change, individually and communally. Knowing that forces beyond our control are pulling us together, we can resist the voices that seek to divide us, making us arrogant, cynical, or afraid. Always, the still, small voice inside aligns our thoughts and deeds with the quiet power that uplifts us.

Fifty years of research have taught us to be humble as we try to predict the future. Nature is marvelously complex, and unexpected events have dramatic results. Regardless of our activity, the processes of birth and re-birth, of healing change, will prevail. As we continue to watch and learn from Isle Royale, we must think beyond single species, honoring the interconnectedness of all life, searching for answers while accepting ambiguities.

From the wolf's viewpoint, fearful humans make dangerous neighbors. In just a couple of generations, knowledge has helped us overcome our fear of wolves. When asked to draw a wolf, most of the school children Rolf encounters draw animals with closed mouths, not bared fangs. But other sorts of fears continue to overpower us, sometimes causing paralysis and other times making us violent. Instead of learning all we can about what frightens us, in order to face our fears we invest much effort trying to protect ourselves. Life is a risky business, but we can rejoice in the web of life that inextricably binds all things together. Education will continue to transform us from sheep-like animals that run in a flock (and that wolves cannot resist the temptation to chase) to human beings who act responsibly rather than react violently.

When our "Little Brother" Chris was eight or nine years old, I was helping him with a Cub Scout project, thinking of ways to save the planet. "Stop making war," was Chris' first idea. I tried to steer him in the direction of bicycles or recycling, but he was insistent. I finally got the connection and marveled at the intuitive wisdom of a child who knows violence in any form harms both the planet and its inhabitants. Humans have the ability to recognize our potential for

violence and to detect and resist the voices that would make us afraid and hateful. From the perspective of the wolves of Isle Royale, major players in my favorite circus, the best thing we in the audience can do for them is to get along with each other.

List of Sources

Annin, Peter. *The Great Lakes Water Wars*. Washington, DC: Island Press, 2006.

Baker, Russell. "Best Time To Be Alive." *New York Times Magazine*, April 18, 1999.

Barnett, Lincoln. *The Universe and Dr. Einstein*. New York: New American Library, 1952.

Beard, Daniel Carter. *The American Boy's Handy Book*. 1882; rpt. Boston: Nonpareil Books, 1983.

Campbell, Joseph. *The Power of Myth*. New York: Doubleday, 1988.

A Course in Miracles. Foundation for Inner Peace, 1975.

Eliot, T. S. "Choruses from the Rock," in *Collected Poems* (1909, 1935). New York: Harcourt Brace Jovanovich, 1936.

Fynn. *Mister God, This Is Anna*. New York: Ballantine Books, 1977.

Gibran, Kahlil. *The Prophet*. New York: Alfred A. Knopf, 1965.

Hammarskjöld, Dag. *Markings*. New York: Alfred A. Knopf, 1964.

Joseph, Pat. "'Societies Choose to Fail or Succeed': Looking to History for Today's Survival Strategies." *Sierra Magazine*, 90:3 (May–June 2005), 44, 45.

Moore, Thomas. *Care of the Soul*. New York: Harper Perennial, 1994.

Pascal, Blaise. *Pensées*. 1670.

Peterson, Rolf O. *The Wolves of Isle Royale: A Broken Balance*. Minocqua, WI: Willow Creek Press, 1995; reissued Ann Arbor: U of Michigan Press, 2007.

Pope, Alexander. *Thoughts on Various Subjects*. 1741.

Quinn, Daniel. *Ishmael*. New York: Bantam Books, 1992.

Rahner, Karl. In *Hearts on Fire: Praying with the Jesuits*. Ed. Michael Harter. Chicago: Loyola Press, 2005.

Rohr, Richard. *Radical Grace*. Cincinnati: St. Anthony Messenger Press, 1995.

Saint Exupéry, Antoine de. *Wind, Sand and Stars*. New York: Harcourt Brace Jovanovich, 1967.

Sivertsen, Howard. *Once upon an Isle*. Mt. Horeb, WI: Wisconsin Folk Museum, 1992.

Thoreau, Henry David. *Walden*. New York: Random House, 1950.

Vucetich, J.A., R.O. Peterson, and T.A. Waite. "Raven Scavenging Favours Group Foraging in Wolves." *Animal Behaviour*, 67 (2004): 1117–26.

Vucetich, J.A, and R.O. Peterson. *Ecological Studies of Wolves on Isle Royale*. Houghton, MI: Michigan Technological University, 2008.

Waterman, Jonathan. *Where Mountains Are Nameless*. New York: Norton, 2005.

Williamson, Marianne. *Return to Love: Reflections on the Principles of a Course in Miracles*. New York: HarperCollins, 1992.